PowerSpeaking®

How Ordinary People Can Make Extraordinary Presentations

Frederick Gilbert, Ph.D.

"It's not about perfection. Let 'er rip!"

—Dena Pappas
Mentor

Frederick Gilbert Associates, Inc.
1233 Harrison Avenue
Redwood City, CA 94062
(800) 828-1909

ISBN: 0-9629272-5-2

LCCN: 94-96025

Design, typesetting, and printing services provided by About Books, Inc., 425 Cedar Street, Buena Vista, CO 81211, 800-548-1876.

ATTENTION CORPORATIONS, COLLEGES, AND PROFESSIONAL ORGANIZATIONS: Quantity discounts are available on bulk purchases of this book for educational purposes or fund raising. Special books or book excerpts can also be created to fit specific needs. For information, please contact Frederick Gilbert Associates, Inc., 1233 Harrison Avenue, Redwood City, California 94062 or call (800) 828-1909.

Table of Contents

Introduction 1
The Myth of Perfection 3
The Three Essentials of Speaking 5

The Substance of Speaking

Content is Everything (Almost*) 11
Can Stories *Really* Persuade People? 18
Death-Defying Rescue Saves Speaker 21
Should You Use Stories?
   Only If You Want Impact! 23
Finding the Perfect Image 26
Using Humor 27
In Praise of Profanity 29
Tips on Openings, Humor and Structure 31
Women's Language, Women's Power 34
How to Do Introductions 39
To Improve Your Speeches, Do Research 41

The Style of Speaking

Style Essentials 47
The Snooze Factor: How to Beat It 54
Of Liars and Speakers 57
The Perils of Adrenalin 59

With a Little Help from Your Friends 63

What Speakers Can Learn from Actors 66

Stage Fright? Change Your Face! 69

The Sound of Your Voice 71

Practice Makes P~~erfect~~ Better 74

Dress and Appearance 76

High-Heel Horror 78

The Staging of Speaking

Working with Hotels:

   Advice from the Experts 83

Staging with E's 86

A Speaker's Nightmare:

   The Out-of-Control Audience 88

Dealing with Hostile Questions 91

Q & A Strategies 94

How to Moderate a Panel Discussion 96

The Athenian Myth 99

Audience Satisfaction 101

Listening to Your Audience 104

The Power of Speaking

From the Trenches to the Podium—

   What Speakers Can Learn from the General . 109

Speakers Tell It Like It Is 112

Don't Even Think About Getting It "Right" . . . 117

Quick Tips for Speakers 120

Peak Performance Under Pressure 122

The Business of Speaking

The Seven Myths of Business Speaking 127
Welcome to the '90s:
    Speaking to a Culturally Diverse Audience . . 132
Corporate Employee Meetings with Pizzazz! . . . 136
Promoting Yourself and Your Business
    Through Speaking 139
Business Speaking: Boredom or Impact? 142
Acting vs. Speaking 144
PowerSpeaking® Helps Land Big Sale 146

The Technology of Speaking

The Technical Presentation 151
Computer-Generated Graphics:
    Use with Caution 156
Let's Not Get Lost in the Technology 158
Visual Aids Do Not a Presentation Make 160
Graphically Speaking 164
"They Didn't Want Statistics . . ." 165
"Oh Yeah? . . . Says Who?"
    Things We Know *For Sure* About Speaking . . 166
The Impact of Music 171
Microphones:
    What You Don't Know *Can* Hurt You 172
How to Record Your Presentations 175

The Biology of Speaking

A Speaker's Diet 181
Blood Sugar and Your Performance 183
Care and Feeding of Your Voice 185

The Future of Speaking

PowerSpeaking® for Kids 191

How to Get More Practice 193

Diana Bock Knocks Their Socks Off! 195

PowerSpeaking® First Graders? Absolutely! . . . 197

The Soul of Speaking

Divine Dissatisfaction 203

Technique + Soul = Impact 206

Stand Up and Speak Out: Spontaneous Speaking
   The Oratorical Equivalent of Bungee Jumping . 208

Dad Was a Speaker 212

The Power of the Hero's Journey 215

Using Video to Capture Family History 218

The Truth Is in the Attic 221

"Would You Say a Few Words About Dan?" . . . 222

A Living Memorial for Lauren 224

Contributors' Biographies 226

Introduction

From passion to technology, from soul to strategy—it's all here. In *PowerSpeaking®: How Ordinary People Can Make Extraordinary Presentations*, you will learn the building blocks of excellent presentations while you explore the lofty heights of your own communication powers. You will learn (or be reminded) of the importance of *passion* and *conviction* in delivering any speech or presentation. And you will be introduced to my driving philosophy about the art and practice of public speaking: *It's not about perfection.*

My goal with this book is to free the great speaker within you. I've done approximately 5,000 presentations in my lifetime, and the most important things I've learned over the years about what makes "great speakers" are: they focus on what they care about, they take risks, they avoid perfectionism—and they practice, practice, practice.

What do you care about? What do you want to tell the world (or your department) about politics? about product development? about injustice? about technology? The list can go on and on. The point is—and you'll hear this echoing throughout the book—the speeches and presentations that move us, that enlighten, that help us do a better job, that effect change, are given to us by people who care deeply about what they're saying and who have worked hard to make their delivery live up to their passion.

The material in this book was written over an eight-year period and some articles were originally published in our quarterly newsletter to clients. While the book has been designed to give you the essentials in a format that is easy to read, *PowerSpeaking®: How Ordinary People Can Make Extraordinary Presentations*, offers a breadth of information that is unequaled in the how-to market on this subject (and I've read them all!). The book—one third of which is written by other professionals and colleagues—begins with three main sections, which mirror the three-point training model we've developed: the substance, style and staging of speaking. From there we take you on a journey that spans the power, the business, the technology, the biology, the future and the soul of speaking. Furthermore, the information you will receive is truly leading edge—no endless lists of predictable do's and don'ts here!

The book is designed to be read straight through and the chapters build sequentially. Depending on your particular interest or need, however, you may want to skip around. If, for example, you are a newer, inexperienced speaker, you might begin with chapters one to five. If you're a seasoned speaker looking for fine-tuning, start with chapters six to nine. If you're primarily a speaker on technical topics, start with chapter eight.

Of course this journey through the art and practice of speaking has an end: you, in front of an audience (again and again). However you approach this material, I'm confident your next audience will experience your best speech ever.

Frederick Gilbert, Ph.D.

The Myth of Perfection

Years ago I learned a powerful lesson about speaking from—of all people—a music teacher. She taught me that expressing ourselves is not about being perfect. It's about the courage to make mistakes.

Like many people, my childhood attempts to learn music had been painful affairs. I remember, for example, a piano teacher, Miss Terwilliger, who would rap my fingers with a pencil and scold me for not practicing. At 37, though, I resolved to try music again—this time with the tenor saxophone.

It began at a music store in San Rafael, California. My saxophone teacher was a platinum blond named Dena Pappas. She was the lead player in a group called "The All-Girl Rock and Roll Band" that played at The Condor Club in San Francisco's North Beach.

At my first meeting with Dena, she asked what I wanted to play. I said, "The tenor saxophone." She asked, "Then why do you have that little alto?" "Because my other teacher said I wouldn't have enough breath control for a tenor," I replied hesitantly. "What crap. Here, try this," and she handed me her huge, gold, rhinestone-studded, Selmer Mark VI tenor saxophone. When I played the scales, the low notes made my guts vibrate. I knew I was home. This is what I came for.

As I played the scales, I made lots of mistakes. Dena said, "Hey, keep going. Sounds great." Her encouragement was infectious. She cared more about the feeling than about perfection. This attitude prevailed throughout all my lessons with Dena.

Finally, I had mastered a song, "When Johnny Comes Marching Home." As I practiced, Dena and I stood side by side playing together. I'd miss one note after another, and she'd yell: "It's not about perfection. Let 'er rip!" and off we'd go. Finally, I was having fun with music. Eat your heart out Miss Terwilliger.

Dena Pappas knew that learning a new skill takes courage and encouragement. When it comes to speaking, the same philosophy applies. In manufacturing we may strive to "get it right the first time." In speaking, however, perfection is not only unattainable, it shouldn't even be our goal.

The next time you get up to speak and feel those butterflies in the stomach, the dry mouth and the sweaty palms, remember Dena Pappas. Imagine her spirit in the room. Her saxophone blaring. Hear her shouting in your ear, "It's not about perfection. Let 'er rip!"

The Three Essentials
of Speaking

Imagine yourself standing with over 200,000 others on the steps and grounds of the Lincoln Memorial on August 28, 1963, as Martin Luther King repeats the hypnotic refrain: "I have a dream!" You are swept away by the power of the message and the impact of that historical moment.

All the key ingredients for the making of an unforgettable speech were there: the substance, the style and the staging. All speakers who must make an impact on their audiences need to pay attention to these three factors.

Substance—This is the content of your message, the heart of why you are speaking. It is the core message, the opening and closing, the key points, the stories, the humor and the passion.

Style—Style is the *way* in which the content is delivered. It is the sum of all the myriad techniques that differentiate the pro from the beginner: stance, movement, gestures, voice, pause and eye interaction.

Staging—Most beginning speakers and many seasoned professionals, overlook this area. Think of staging as all the subtle details the audience is usually unaware of—but that can ruin an otherwise outstanding presentation: the quality of the PA system (all 200,000 people could hear King's message loud and clear); the speaker's familiarity with AV equipment, i.e., knowing how to turn the overhead projector on and off—and keeping it off when not in use; the effective use of visual aids; the seating arrangement; the use of handout material in a nondisruptive way; the lighting and so forth. The other aspect of staging is dealing with audience reactions and behavior.

Often, in business and technical presentations, the speaker is so concerned with substance, i.e., getting the facts and numbers right, that the impact is lost. With little attention paid to style or staging, the speech can be flat. The audience may be overwhelmed with detail and soon lose interest.

On the other hand, overemphasis on style can result in an audience being temporarily dazzled, but "an hour later feeling hungry for content." An overemphasis on staging may leave an audience impressed with the show; but they won't feel connected with the presenter. Some corporate high-tech road shows spend small fortunes on flashy models, 35mm computer-driven slide shows and videotape presentations, but little on the presentation skills of the speaker. Yet in spite of the dazzling show, it is the confidence, persuasiveness and believability of the real, live human being who is presenting the show that will make the prospects feel comfortable with the product and the company.

Business, sales and technical presenters, then, would do well to seek a balance between substance, style and staging. Content alone will not persuade their listeners. Remember what made Martin Luther King's speech memorable—in addition to moving content—was world-class delivery (style) and excellent staging. He had all three of the essential ingredients. So can you!

In the following three chapters, we'll explore substance, style and staging.

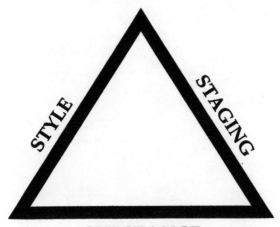

SUBSTANCE

STYLE
- Eye Interaction
- Pause
- Voice
- Gestures
- Movement
- Stance
- Dress

STAGING
- Lighting
- Room Arrangement
- Visual Aids
- Props/Handouts
- Audience Involvement
- Q & A Sessions
- Audience Control

SUBSTANCE
- Core Message
- Key Points
- Evidence
- Humor
- Stories
- Examples
- Openings/Closings

The Substance of Speaking

> "I've enjoyed hearing speakers who combine humor and anecdotes with their technical stuff. I remember what they've said. They entertain as well as convey information."
>
> —Richard Eaton
> Hewlett-Packard

As Richard Eaton notes, the purpose of a presentation is to "convey information." He also observes that when a speaker balances data with anecdotes, he'll remember what they said. To be effective, your substance needs to be well organized. When it is, the audience will stay with you. Using stories will help them remember.

Presentations are far more than just data. In this chapter we'll look at how to organize information around a core message, how to open and close, how to use humor and the importance of your language.

Content is Everything (Almost*)

You've been asked to speak because you're an expert or have some special knowledge. In everyday business and technical presentations, content is "stage center." It is the base of the PowerSpeaking® triangle. How the content is organized is critical to audience attention and retention.

The first step is to find out who is in your audience. What do they need to know? Your content should be tailored to meet their needs.

Core Message

The next step is to decide what is the essence of your talk. What one or two ideas do you want people to leave with? Keep in mind that two days after hearing your talk, people will have forgotten 95% of what you said. Make sure they remember your main idea. We call it the "core message."

To be effective, a core message is short and it's repeated. Martin Luther King, for example, said "I have a dream" nine times in the seven minutes it took to deliver that speech. The following examples are familiar core messages.

Style and staging are also critical.

Core Messages from Advertising

"It's the real thing."—*Coca Cola*

"I love what you do for me."—*Toyota*

"Don't leave home without it."—*American Express*

"Quality is Job 1."—*Ford*

Core Messages from Speeches

"I have a dream."—*Martin Luther King, Jr.*

"First, commit the nation; then commit the troops."
—*H. Ross Perot* (Gulf War Speech, Press Club)

"Read my lips: no new taxes!"—*George Bush*

Note that a topic, i.e., "Quality," is not a core message. However the sentence: "Quality is our competitive advantage" is a core message. For example:

Topic	*Core Message*
Customer satisfaction	"Customer satisfaction is our top priority."
Quality	"Quality is our competitive advantage."
Corporate child care	"Corporate child care is a benefit to the child, employee and to the company."

Core messages and key points must be driven home in a number of ways. Here are some techniques to make your speech more memorable.

1. Verbal emphasis (For example: "Now get this . . .")
2. Three distributed repetitions
3. Immediate repetition early in the speech
4. Speaking slowly (half normal rate)
5. Immediate repetitions late in the speech
6. Pauses
7. Gestures

Cited in *Understanding Persuasion*, Third Edition, Raymond S. Ross, Prentice Hall, Englewood Cliffs, NJ, 1990, p. 162.

> *"A speech is like a symphony. It can have three movements, but it must have one dominant melody."*
> —Sir Winston Churchill

Key Points

Key points are the way you convince the listener of the value of the core message. Key points may be either analytical or narrative. Analytical key points consist of data, statistics, research results, etc. Narrative key points may be stories, illustrations or examples. Analytical key points persuade the mind while narrative key points persuade the heart. Based on audience preferences and needs, you may emphasize different types of key points.

To enhance the impact of your message, keep the number of key points small. People may be able to recall three or four key points, but it's unlikely they will be able to remember ten or twelve.

No Test

Remember in college classes how you wrote down everything the professor said no matter how deadly boring it was. Why did you do that? Because it could show up on the test. Fear was the great motivation.

Many presenters still use that model in their business presentations. They erroneously believe there is some outside force, like the fear of the grade, that will cause the audience to pay attention. The sobering reality is that most of your audience is daydreaming most of the time. During your presentation, they may be thinking about a wide variety of things: phone calls they need to return, reports that are due, the Little League game tonight, the Hawaiian vacation next week, etc., etc.

Your presentation competes with all of that for their attention.

One defense you have for fading attention is tight organization that is easy to follow. Have a succinct and repeated core message and have only a few key points. If there is massive detail you want the audience to take away, consider giving it to them as a handout and keep the actual presentation material bold and easy to follow. Presentations are not the forum for a "data dump." Keep it simple and you will enhance attention and retention.

Of Pilots and Speakers

Eighty-six percent of airplane crashes occur during take-off or landing. The same is true for speakers. If the opening is slow, tentative and boring, the audience will decide early on to mentally check out. It is hard to win them back once that has happened.

Similarly, the closing sequence gives a speaker a last chance to have impact, to drive the point home or to help the audience remember the key points. Even a mediocre presentation may be revived with a strong, memorable close. Yet some speakers do not plan a powerful closing sequence. They just wind down, stop talking and thank the audience.

Here are some ideas to help you lift off and land with confidence the next time you speak.

Openings

Your opening is your first and most critical opportunity to grab and hold the audience's interest. The opening is also a time of high-level nervousness and stress. If your audience senses your hesitation or nervousness, they may lose interest. You, of course, respond to their reaction by feeling even less confident. Things go downhill from there.

What to do? Capture and hold their attention by coming on full-force. Learn your opening at the "muscle memory" level. In other words, charge through your nervousness by *overlearning* the opening.

Powerful Opening Techniques

- ► Humor (not a joke)
- ► Story
- ► Quotation
- ► Audience participation
- ► Questions (literal or rhetorical)
- ► Startling statement/fact/statistic

Audiences pay closer attention to, and are more likely to remember, what happens at the beginning and at the end of your talk. State your core message loud and clear at the beginning and again during the summary. Of course, you should also mention it in the body of the talk.

Closings

Have a well-rehearsed, powerful close. Be ready to transition to the close at any time. This will help you control your time and give you a strong, ready exit should you need it.

Powerful Closing Techniques

- ► Summary
- ► Core message
- ► Call to action
- ► Story
- ► Quotation
- ► Humor

As author and speaker Judith Briles says, "Leave 'em laughing, leave 'em crying, leave 'em thinking—but don't just leave 'em."

Your openings and closings take only five to ten percent of your presentation time, yet they have a very strong impact on the success of your speech. To avoid being a speaker who doesn't have enough power to lift off, or who runs out of gas a mile from the runway, try the techniques we've outlined. Your message will be remembered if the take-off and landing are smooth.

Presentation Plan

On the next page you will see our model for how to organize a talk. It's in an oval shape to reflect what might be called the speaker's journey. We set up the opening sequences, move down into the body of the talk with the key points and come back up through the conclusion. The challenge that we opened with may be resolved in the action step (what we want people to do). And so we end where we began.

If you are using visual aids such as overhead transparencies, it's a good idea to keep the overhead projector off during the opening and closing sequences. This focuses attention more on you and your core message for greater impact.

The following segments of this chapter explore other content issues including stories, humor, language and topic research.

PRESENTATION PLAN

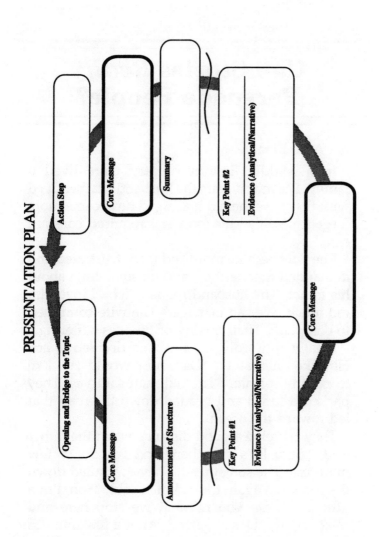

Can Stories *Really* Persuade People?

An Arab Parable:

In a Middle Eastern country there lived a family. For many years the husband's father lived with them. As the old man aged he became more forgetful, spilled his food and required constant care.

The wife became more and more frustrated and demanded that her husband do something about his father. The husband replied, "No. I love him too much. We can manage." The wife continued to complain. Their quality of life was suffering.

Finally and sadly, the husband decided to act. He asked his father, "Dad, how would you like to go on a picnic?" The old man said yes. They packed a lunch and headed down the road that led toward the ocean.

They traveled a good distance when the father said, "Son, let's stop here and rest for a few minutes." The son agreed. They continued down the road and again the old man said, "Son, I'm a little tired. Do you mind if we stop here and rest?" Again the son agreed. After a few minutes the old man said, "I'm ready to go on." They

18

continued farther. The son was feeling guilty. His heart was breaking as he walked along with his father. Finally, the son said, "Dad, let's stop here." The old man replied, "Do you mind if we go a little farther down the road toward the ocean?" The son asked why and the old man responded, "You know the first place we stopped? That was where my father took his father. The second place we stopped was where I took my father. This is where you have taken me. I wanted to see where your son will take you."

A few moments later, the son said, "Dad, let's go home."

Several months ago in a PowerSpeaking® workshop, Joe Gammal used this story to persuade the group of the importance of caring for our elders. The story was not original with Joe. His own father, Albert Gammal, had used the story many years ago when he was a representative in the Massachusetts State Legislature.

The bill being debated would have excused people from financial responsibility for the care of their aging parents, regardless of their ability to pay. Under the bill, the state would care for all the elderly, even those from wealthy families. Albert Gammal felt there was a moral issue involved, that the state would be setting a precedent in ceasing to acknowledge that children have a responsibility to their parents, as parents have a responsibility to their children.

As Representative Gammal spoke, the audience grew silent. As he told this story, which his father had brought with him when he immigrated from their native Syria, he became choked with emotion. When he finished, there was not a sound in the chamber. When the vote was called, the only "aye" was from the bill's author.

People are persuaded by more than facts and statistics. They are also moved by stories. Your well-developed and delivered stories will add heart and persuasion to your next presentation.

Death-Defying Rescue
Saves Speaker

You want your audience to feel the urgency of the situation. You want them to take action. Yet, you are no orator. What to do?

This situation faced Jerry Davis, vice president of Worldwide Client Support at Network Equipment Technologies (N.E.T.) in Redwood City, California. Jerry was scheduled to deliver an important presentation to the entire company live and on video at the "All Hands Meeting." Although highly regarded in his position, "confident speaker" was not the way he'd describe himself. In fact, speaking always terrified him.

When Jerry and I first met to work on his talk, he was not clear what he wanted to say. He felt strongly, though, that he needed to get people fired up about the front-end process of the product life cycle. While field engineers had been doing an outstanding job of handling problems at customer sites—and should get recognition for that—he wanted people to collaborate better at the early stages of product design.

An image came to mind as we talked. Several months earlier I noticed a newspaper photograph of a near tragedy. At an air show in Oregon a wing-walker had slipped and fallen off a biplane. As he hung precariously by a life line, the plane flew slowly down the runway (about 80 miles per hour). A quick-witted ground crew rounded up a pickup truck and heavy-gauge wire cutters. The truck sped along the runway until it could position itself under the helpless stunt man. The life line was cut and he fell safely into the truck bed. Certain death was avoided. A dramatic story of a process that had gone awry.

I asked Jerry if that was like what happens when field people have to act quickly and heroically to fix problems at customer sites. The image fit perfectly. What made the image ideal for Jerry is that he is also a stunt pilot and most of the company knew that.

Jerry worked on relating the story to the product life cycle. His enthusiasm for the talk grew. He told the audience the dramatic wing-walker story, then added:

"N.E.T. does an Olympic job of bailing us out of problems after they occur. But we don't do a good enough job on the front end. I can't buy enough pickup trucks to keep solving these problems. I need your help on the product life cycle. I apologize if the front end work isn't exciting, but frankly I don't know if my heart will take many more of these."

His talk was short and to the point. His meaning was clear. The sense of urgency hit everyone. Afterwards, people told Jerry they really understood what he meant. For weeks later there was talk around the company of wing-walkers and pickup trucks. The right image, for the right speaker, for the right talk, had made all the difference.

For your next important speech, take time to find the right image. It will make the talk more fun to develop and easier to deliver. More importantly, your audience will get your message on the wings of metaphor.

Should You Use Stories? Only If You Want Impact!

Recently, I gave a short luncheon presentation. I began with the story of Dena Pappas, my saxophone teacher and her advice, "Let 'er rip!" After the presentation, a woman came up to say she enjoyed the session and that, in fact, she'd heard me speak before. She wasn't sure where and she actually hadn't recognized me, but she remembered the Dena Pappas story. Her comment reminded me again of the power of stories.

If you are not now using stories in your presentations, you are missing a powerful link between your content and your audience. In fact, research has shown that stories have stronger impact than quantitative data in some forms of corporate communications (Martin and Powers in *Psychological Foundations of Organizational Behavior*, 1983).

Stories replacing corporate policy manuals? That's the goal of David Armstrong, vice president of Armstrong International, a worldwide manufacturer of precision mechanical equipment. In his book, *Managing By Storying Around*, he shares company stories he has used to communicate the company's core values.

Where can you find stories that will have the strongest impact? The best source is personal experience. You can also use other people's stories if they can be made to fit your presentation goals.

Many speakers at the 1992 Democratic Convention used stories. Bill Clinton especially needed to tell stories about his life to let the audience get to know him and to help counteract the "character issues" he'd been fighting in the primaries. Perhaps his most effective story was about working in his grandfather's store as a boy. He concluded the story with the lesson learned: "My grandfather had a grade-school education. But in that country store he taught me more about equality in the eyes of the Lord than all my professors at Georgetown."

Do stories have to be "true?" Yes—at least in intent. It helps in the telling. For example, my saxophone teacher story is essentially true. I can actually see pictures in my mind of what happened as I tell it. But Dena may not have said, "Let 'er rip"; I don't remember her exact words. The point is, the spirit of the story is absolutely true.

Are there times not to use stories? Obviously, in some types of technical presentations, stories may be inappropriate. Master storyteller and presentations coach Robert Fish works a lot with technical presenters. He notes that while they are often hesitant to use stories, they will sometimes use metaphors or analogies to get their ideas across in nontechnical ways. Once you've decided to use stories, where do you start? Robert's advice is to start by listening to other people tell stories. Be analytical. Be aware of gestures, body movement, eye contact, use of the voice, etc. The next step is to try your stories out informally on friends for effect and for rehearsal.

According to Robert, beginning "tellers" make two errors. "The most common mistake of storytellers is adding too much detail and dragging it out far too long," says Robert. Another problem is being too timid. He advises, "Take risks in delivery. Use dialogue and let your voice reflect the emotion of the characters."

Now you are ready to use stories. You may be surprised at the impact they have on your audiences. Oh, by the way, did I tell you about the time when . . .

Finding the Perfect Image

Recently a participant in our two-day Power-Speaking® program described her job responsibilities by using an overhead transparency of a three-ring circus. The effect was stunning. She got the idea (and the graphic image) while reading a bedtime story about the circus to her daughter the night before.

Where do you get ideas for your presentations? In the shower? While exercising? While watching a movie? The most unlikely places or activities can generate powerful speech material.

In Search of Excellence co-author Tom Peters lamented in a recent newspaper column that he sees so many business travelers cranking out the numbers on their laptop computers during cross-country flights. Big breakthroughs and much-needed creative solutions are more likely to come from letting the mind wander, says Peters. He recommends decidedly non-business sources like Sherlock Holmes books, *Zen and the Art of Motorcycle Maintenance* or even the Clint Eastwood grade B in-flight movie.

As a speaker you may find just the right image to ignite your audience's commitment to your ideas by going outside conventional sources for your material. Your presentations are too important to get bogged down in the ordinary. Dare to be creative.

Using Humor

"Laughter is the shortest distance between two people."
—Victor Borge
Comedian

After booking me for a keynote speech at his association's annual Christmas get-together, the meeting planner said: "Last May, at our state-wide two-day conference, one so-called 'motivational speaker' turned out to be a plastic surgeon who lectured us on the joys of doing tummy tucks and removing crow's feet. He included detailed medical slides. The members were outraged. Many stormed out. "I'm still getting criticism about it," he lamented.

I asked him how many people at the December meeting would have heard the surgeon. He said well over two-thirds. That was all I needed. I knew I had my opening.

My opening line was: "When Bill asked me to address you today, he said you were interested in motivational strategies. I assured him he selected the right speaker. As an expert in the field, I can tell you enthusiastically that I have the answer to your queries. The motivational strategy for the 90s is . . . (long pause) . . . plastic surgery." The audience roared and we were off to a good start.

Humor is an invaluable asset to the speaker or business presenter. It breaks the ice, builds rapport and reduces tension. It opens people up so they can hear your message.

The best type of humor is that which grows naturally out of the situation or out of your own experience. Art Linkletter once addressed the inmates at San Quentin during their annual track and field competition. His opening line was; "The warden asked me to announce that the pole vaulting event has been cancelled." It brought the house down.

Humorous real-life situations or stories that can be adapted for your audience will likely work better than canned jokes. Try out funny material on several different groups of friends to make sure it works and to fine tune it.

Well-crafted humorous stories from your own experience will warm up the audience and help to relax you. Skip the jokes though . . . unless you're Bill Cosby.

In Praise of Profanity

"I'll be *damned* if I'll let anyone with a smirk and a sneer discredit the honor, service, accountability and competence of George Bush." With that line, former president Gerald Ford brought the 1988 Republican National Convention screaming to their feet. It was the brightest moment of an otherwise ordinary, too predictable convention.

It made me reflect on the unwritten, though often articulated rule in many speaking organizations that advises speakers to never swear in a speech. I think it is time for us to re-examine that advice. Swearing can add intensity and emotional honesty—not to mention color. Of course, I'm not recommending that we use those big multi-syllable words. The impact, though, of what we might call "lightweight" profanity can be dramatic.

Nationally known speaker, Zig Zigler, commented at a National Speakers Association Convention that he didn't enjoy hearing "barnyard language" from a speaker. I agree with him that raunchy sexual stories have no place in corporate or association platform speaking. Las Vegas, perhaps—but not where most of us work. But swearing to underscore a strongly felt position, that is okay with me.

"But wait," you say. "Swearing may offend someone in my audience." One of the saddest comments I ever heard was from a colleague who proudly proclaimed that his material had been so sanitized it offended no one. I hope that when I'm lowered in the ground they don't chisel on my tombstone: "Here Lies A Speaker Who Offended No One." I'd rather it said: "Here Lies A Speaker Who Told It Like It Was. He Won Some, He Lost Some."

Life is not one big sales rally of good news and unlimited opportunity. As speakers we need to be in touch with the dark side, too. We are at our finest when we inspire from strong conviction. And occasionally, as we get ourselves and the audience worked up about our topic, swearing may actually enhance, not hurt our message.

> *"Show me a guy who says 'heck' and 'darn' and I'll show you a guy who would kick a dog."*
> —Bill Gove, Professional Speaker

Yes, some people may be offended. It is a calculated risk. Is the intensity and emotional honesty worth it? Each of us will have to decide for ourselves. Swearing hasn't hurt Tom Peters' career. If you've seen him in person you know how he adds intensity with profanity. Audiences don't seem too offended: his calendar is booked for three years out. People like to see speakers light themselves on fire on stage. That's what he does. It's not the swearing *per se* that makes him popular, it's the passion about an important topic.

I hope we aspire to nothing less. It is time to re-evaluate this sacred cow. In the words of Elbert Hubbard, "A great orator is inspired by many, but a copy of none. No prudent person ever made a multitude change its mind. Oratory is indiscretion set to music."

Tips on Openings,
Humor and Structure

Contributed by Patricia Fripp, CPAE

Getting Started

You must get to the point. Grab the audience's attention. For example, make a startling statement.

For a recent speech to the National Speakers Association, I walked out and immediately started building a word picture: "Columbus, Ohio, December, zero degrees, 2,000 people trudging through the snow to hear four speakers . . ."

Do not waste your audience's time. I heard a speaker at the Sales and Marketing Executives Association meeting in San Francisco. He had one hour to talk, was twenty minutes late in starting (beyond his control), but had to finish on time. He started with: how nice it was to be in San Francisco, how great the weather was, how he loves our restaurants. Who cares? I did not race across town to hear him talk about weather and restaurants.

Tape your talks and as you listen, ask the question, "Who cares?" after every statement or segment of material. It is a great way to see if you are saying anything of value.

31

Be Funny . . . Maybe

Humor can add a lot to your speech, but it needs to fit you and your topic. You may ask yourself, ". . . but am I funny?" A friend from AT&T called me one evening at 10:45 PM. He said, "My boss is giving a speech tomorrow. He needs a joke." "No problem," I replied. "What is the theme of the talk and what are his key points?" I told him every joke I knew that might fit into his format. Nothing worked. Finally, I asked, "Is your boss funny?" "Well . . . not really," he responded. My advice to him was: "Don't get him to be funny. Get him to be inspiring." Looking through my reference books, I found quotes that fit his points much better than humor.

If humor is appropriate to your speech and to you, use it. Look for material that grows naturally out of your content—rather than jokes that may or may not fit.

Putting It All Together

A good outline for both beginning and professional speakers is the Alcoholics Anonymous format: "This is where I am, this is where I was, this is how I got here." It is a great structure because it is very easy to remember.

One of the best talks I ever heard was several years ago in Canada. Art Linkletter came on at about 10:00 PM. He was the sixth speaker, with a sound system that did not work well. People were nervous, uncomfortable and fidgety. Yet, he gave a talk that was so great, I can remember what he said years later.

He started out his humorous introduction with stories of the kids that were on his show. Then he said, "My life has been in three parts: when I was poor, when I was rich and famous—and after my daughter died of a drug overdose. Since then, I have donated my time to help other people understand these problems.

The last third has been the most satisfying." With the AA format and the clear outline, the audience could tell exactly where he was going.

Another example of considering your audience happened recently when I received a phone call from a woman in Yuma, Arizona. She said, "We have a mutual friend, Ernie Choenis. I am giving a speech in three weeks and he said you would send me one of your tapes. I could learn what to say and give the talk." "It doesn't actually work just like that, but tell me, who are you addressing?" I asked. "The Yuma Board of Realtors," she said. I asked, "Why have they invited you to speak?" She responded, "I have been very successful in the real estate industry."

I suggested she use the AA outline. This is where I am: Last year I sold $18 million in real estate in a slow market where the average sale was $50,000. This is where I was: Eight years ago when I got my license, I had never sold anything but Girl Scout cookies, and didn't do that very well. This is how I got here: First, I . . ." She used the outline and reported later that the talk was a big hit.

Your outline should be simple. This way you can remember what you intend to say and your audience can remember what they heard. I speak the way I cook: how it turns out is the way I intended it to be!

Women's Language, Women's Power

Contributed by Mary McGlynn

It is budget time. Several decision-makers watch as a woman walks to the front, smiles and begins her presentation.

> "Thank you *so* much for coming. I'm *so* pleased to see your *bright* faces. I have a *wonderful* budget that I know you'll *really* like because it's going to be *terribly* important to our division."

Imagine the same scene, but this time a woman, aware of her speech patterns, is presenting to the Board of Directors.

> "Thank you. I'm pleased to present our new budget. It will allow us to reach our goals but still help us control expenses. Let's look at it."

Women communicate differently than men. We are more polite. We qualify what we say. We appear indecisive because we ask for permission or add questions to the end of our statements. We use "women only" words. The result? Women are not taken as seriously in business and in everyday communication and we undermine our communication process. Let's

34

take a look at some of the ineffective patterns women use and consider stronger alternatives.

Problem Language

Are you using "women only" adjectives and adverbs in your speech? For example, charming, adorable, lovely, sweet and cute are words that few men use. Adverbs such as so, really, terribly, quite, awfully and simply do not add to understanding, but instead differentiate female from male communication. We trivialize our intent when we use words that are weak and/or irrelevant.

Tag Questions or Reflections

Let's look at examples of some statements with tag questions.

▶ "It sure is cold, don't you think?"

▶ "It will be done by Friday?" (with an upward inflection)

▶ "I really presented that clearly, didn't I?"

Ending with a question gives away the certainty, the power. With rising inflection or a "tag question," a statement falls between the cracks: is it a request for information or is it a statement? Such a language pattern gives the impression that you're saying:

▶ "I'm not sure of my facts."

▶ "I need to be liked and want your approval."

▶ "I want to do something but I'll change my mind if you don't approve."

In simplified (and overgeneralized) terms: men command by making a statement; women request through indirect statements in hopes for approval.

Politeness

What are little girls made of? "Sugar and spice and everything nice." A silly childhood rhyme, true, but it illustrates the notion that women exemplify our ideal morality. As a polite creature who can empathize, concur and accommodate, we reduce our social status and give away our power. We are caretakers, not leaders.

According to a recent Toastmaster Magazine article, women ask 70% of the questions in order to "bring others out."

Imagine a woman manager making a request of her secretary: "Will you please type this for me as soon as possible, okay?" The secretary is doing her boss a favor by typing the document. I am not suggesting that it is better to be rude or dominating, but rather, women must choose words that exhibit directness and clarity.

Interruptions

"Snakes and snails and puppy dogs' tails," are what little boys are made of. Men have language patterns that affect women, too.

- ▸ Men dominate conversations.
- ▸ Men speak at greater lengths.
- ▸ Men are more likely to interrupt conversations.

A recent study showed that when women are in conversation with other women, or when men are talking to men, there are about equal interruptions. In a mixed group, all politeness disappears. Men make 96% of all interruptions.

It is also true that if a woman is speaking and is interrupted by a man, she is usually silenced. Even if a woman tries to get the floor again, she probably won't succeed. In our benevolence, we weaken our leadership roles and even give up some of our self-esteem.

These language patterns communicate self-doubt and uncertainty. Although this is predominantly a female problem, men are not immune to the weak language trap. Whether used by males or females, the patterns are destructive.

How To Develop Powerful Language

Being aware of our language patterns is an enormous step. There are many ways to do this.

Tape-recording—Tape-record your conversations in a business meeting or on the phone. Then analyze your language for patterns that trivialize communication.

Videotaping—If you have a major presentation coming up, rehearse on video. There is no better way to make behavioral changes. As a "third party" watching the video, you can check for verbal patterns, body language and self-confidence. Modify your word-use to create the greatest impact.

Interruptions—When interrupted, politely, but firmly, and with a slightly raised voice, indicate that you would like to finish your statement and then proceed. Don't automatically give in! Believe in your right to "have the floor."

Self-Concept—More and more women are becoming aware that self-deprecating behavior is the result of low self-esteem. If your patterns undermine your credibility, be willing to look at your self-concept. Counseling, workshops and presentation skills seminars are all available options.

Look and Listen—Take some time to make changes by studying those people who are effective and dynamic communicators. What do they do? How do they present information? Contrast their success with someone who is not a strong presenter. Incorporate those successful behaviors into your own repertoire.

Summary—Women don't have to communicate less effectively than men. Awareness is the key. Style can change. The results for you will be greater self-confidence, stronger impact and a more dynamic presentation.

How to Do Introductions

Picture this: you're at a large convention to introduce one of your company's new products. You're not on the agenda to speak, but you have been asked to introduce the speaker. How are you going to do it in an effective, professional way? Our model will help.

A proper introduction will establish rapport with the audience, build audience enthusiasm for the speaker, establish the speaker's credibility and make the speaker feel welcome. There are two equally critical components of introductions: verbal and nonverbal.

The Verbal Component

- ▶ *Topic*—Tell the audience what the topic will be.

- ▶ *Interest*—Relate the topic to the audience's interests.

- ▶ *Speaker*—Give the speaker's background and qualifications to speak on the topic.

- ▶ *Name*—Say the name at the end of the introduction.

The Nonverbal Component

- ▶ *Position*—Have the speaker ready to come on.

- ▶ *Clap*—After you say speaker's name, you start clapping. This cues the audience to start applause.

- ▶ **Shake hands**—Welcome the speaker with a handshake and turn over control.
- ▶ **Leave**—Exit the stage area.

Understanding how to give an effective introduction will set the stage at a formal convention, as well as at an informal meeting (simply tone down the nonverbal component a little).

Try this model at your next convention or meeting to warm up the audience and at the same time, raise your own credibility by portraying confidence and organization.

To Improve Your Speeches, Do Research

Contributed by Wally Bock

How do you improve the substance of your speeches? How do you deliver a speech with so much information that people talk about it for months? Research is the key to information power. Here are some tips on how you can put more information power in your speeches.

What Should You Look For?

Good research starts with knowing what to look for. Stories, relevant facts and surprises just seem to make good speeches better.

Look for stories to illustrate your points. Stories are the way that human beings order and remember complex information. Find good stories and examples and you'll help people remember what you said.

Look for little-known facts to provide surprises. People like surprises. Make them say, "I didn't know that!" Historical information about the organization is a good place to find these surprises.

Stay on Top of Your Information

It's easier to prepare for a speech if you don't have to do it all at once. Keeping up with your information

41

prevents last-minute panics and improves your presentations.

Maintain a clipping file on topics that interest you. Use a razor knife or scissors to cut articles out of magazines and newspapers and drop them in the file. Call the folders whatever you like. My folders are: People, Environment and Technology.

Every now and then take them out and look at them all together. I like to do this on business trips when I can spread the articles out on the hotel bed. When they're spread out like that you'll see which topics are showing up frequently, as well as connections you weren't aware of before.

If you're on a computer service like Compuserve or Dow Jones, you can set up electronic clipping files that scan news wires automatically for information you're likely to want. The advantage of picking up articles this way is that you already have them on your computer, so you can use them in your word processor, put them in your notes, etc.

Scan key journals regularly. Look for articles that interest you and cut them out. Add them to your clipping file. This is easy to do if you're connected to an online service, but a couple of hours in the library every month will do the job.

If you're not already online, consider connecting your computer to the online world. Online services will extend your reach for information and for contacts. You'll need a computer, modem, communications software and one or more start-up kits. I recommend you consider Compuserve, America Online, Dow Jones News Retrieval and BRS After Dark as places to start using online services. In my experience, those services provide the most value and are easy to use.

Another trick is to make copies of the tables of contents of key magazines or journals. Put them in a binder and scan them occasionally or when you need to do quick research. You'll get an overview of what's been published recently.

Do Quick Research for Your Specific Presentation

When you have a presentation to do, make it unique by adding relevant, timely information. Start by going back to your files. Look at the articles you've saved. Scan the tables of contents. Make copies of the articles and put them in a project folder for your speech. Review your computerized clipping files, too. This is easiest if you index them, but simple text searches with your word processor will do the trick, too. Gather new information with a quick online search. Services like BRS After Dark are great for this. Pick up names of key authors from the articles you read and from your own network of contacts. Call them up. Ask them for information or ideas. Listen to their stories.

Don't forget to talk to lots of people who'll be in your audience. You'll find out what they want to know, so you can answer their questions. They're a great source of insight and information, too.

Get Your Brain into the Act

As you are gathering information, let your brain do what it does best: make connections and get ideas. Make sure you have a way to capture your ideas and insights. Three techniques that work for me are pocket notepads, pocket tape recorders and pads of Post-It Notes.

Learn to work visually with your material. Most people see connections better that way, probably because you relate ideas "spatially." Working with visuals helps you see connections differently than when you just list things.

Learn techniques like idea mapping or putting your points on Post-Its and outlining by moving them around. Computer programs for outlining and brainstorming can also be a big help because they let you try lots of combinations of ideas before you settle on the best one.

Great information helps make great speeches. Use these tips to enrich your information content. Your audiences will appreciate your effort.

List of Computer Resources for Online Beginners

▶ Compuserve Information Service—800-848-8199

▶ America Online 800-827-6364

▶ BRS 800-955-0906

▶ Dow Jones News Retrieval 800-334-2564

Printed Material to Improve Your Research

▶ *Cyberpower for Speakers, Trainers and Consultants: How to use online research and resources to improve your presentations and your business* by Wally Bock

▶ *Business Information Sources* by Lorna M. Daniells

▶ *The Information Broker's Handbook* by Sue Rugge and Alfred Glossbrenner

The Style of Speaking

> *"If you can't communicate your message, you might as well not have one."*
> —*Geoff Woolhouse, Ph.D.*
> *Space Systems/Loral*

There is a great paradox in speaking. It's the relationship between content and style. Content is the reason you are speaking, yet people will judge your message based on your style. Your style is trivial compared to your message, but the success of your presentation may rise or fall on how you, for example, use your hands. Ridiculous, isn't it?

In this chapter we will look in depth at how you can use all your non-verbal communication tools to enhance the value of your message. When style is done well, it is virtually invisible to your audience.

Style Essentials

You know a lot about the content of your speech. You may even have advanced degrees in your subject. Your nervous mannerisms, though, will drastically reduce your credibility with the audience. The nervousness most likely stems from lack of presentation experience. While you work everyday with your content, chances are you do not stand up and speak about it to groups all that often; hence, the nervousness.

It always makes me sad to see a bright person with an important message go down in flames due to something as "unimportant" as style. It doesn't have to happen. Style is easy to master. This is not rocket science. A few simple things practiced and done well can give you the style power to match the excellence of your message. That's what this chapter is about.

On the following page you will see our "style hierarchy." It summarizes the behaviors speakers must master to be effective in their delivery. For most beginning speakers, all these behaviors operate on "automatic pilot"—that is, beyond conscious control. These speakers have no idea what they're doing with their feet, hands or eye contact. They just do "what comes naturally." In most cases, this is not effective.

You may say, "Well so what? What difference does it make?" If the presenter is pacing back and forth, looking at the floor and fidgeting nervously, the audience begins to doubt the value of the content. This is not fair, but it is reality. The words and numbers do not speak for themselves. The presenter must bring them to life with style.

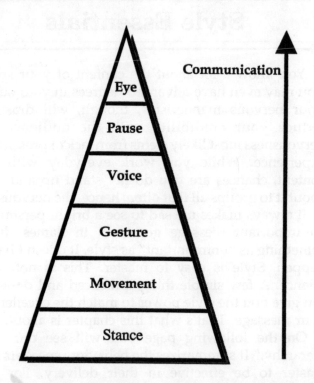

Stance—Nervous energy is often expressed through dancing feet. This is not only distracting to the audience, but it makes the speaker appear ungrounded in what he/she is saying. If you have this problem, imagine your shoes are nailed to the floor. Do not go up on one toe or shift nervously from foot to foot. A balanced stance will make you look stronger in your content.

An effective stance is to have your feet six to eight inches apart, facing forward and your knees slightly bent. Avoid feet held tightly together or too far apart, in what I call the "Mr. Macho" stance.

Movement—While you should keep your feet firmly planted, it also helps to strategically use the space available to you. On the other hand, avoid nervous pacing. It detracts from your message.

Controlled, purposeful movement will actually help the audience follow your content. A good time to move physically is when your content moves to the next point. For example, you might open your presentation in the center of the stage, then move three or four steps to the right for your first key point, cross over to the other side of the stage for your second point and return to the center for your close.

Gestures—Gesturing strongly is perhaps the quickest and easiest way to build your confidence as a speaker. Beginning speakers are far too timid with gestures, fearing they will be too expressive or theatrical if they over-do it. Most have nothing to worry about.

Gestures are a great way to add a visual component to what your words are saying. The audience now gets your message through two channels simultaneously—the auditory and the visual.

Everyone seems to use gestures effectively when speaking comfortably with friends. It's when we stand up to speak and become tense that we get stiff and awkward looking. Let the words dictate your gestures. The addition of gestures to your words will help the audience follow your meaning more clearly. Here are some tips:

> ▸ *Don't cover up the front of your body.* Get out from behind the lectern or overhead projector. Keep your arms at your sides or use them for gestur-

ing. Keeping the front of your body open makes you more vulnerable, less hidden. This actually increases the audience's trust in what you are saying.

▸ *Gesture up and out.* Gesture above the belt and move your arms well away from your body. There are three possible zones for gestures but only one works to your advantage:

Zone I—Arms held in close to the body in the midline; looks timid and apologetic

Zone II—Gestures at shoulder level well away from the body; looks confident, committed and professional

Zone III—Arms fully extended, elbows straight; looks over-blown and phony.

Zone II gestures are appropriate in most speaking situations. Zone I is generally too passive; Zone III is aggressive and insincere.

Using stronger gestures can at first feel artificial and unnatural; yet keep in mind that your audience has been conditioned for years by television. We see confident speakers all the time—and they use bold gestures. Your audience will find such gestures reassuring and they will see you as more believable. Furthermore, these assertive gestures will make you *feel* more confident. It becomes a positive upward spiral.

▸ *Use one-arm gestures.* One-arm (unilateral) gestures are seen by the audience as more confident looking. Two arm (bilateral) gestures make the speaker look more tentative.

▸ *Pockets* "Never put your hands in your pockets!" said my high school speech teacher. "It makes you look too casual," he argued. Nonsense!

Today you will notice that most of the best speakers you see use their pockets. One hand in a pocket makes a speaker look casual, professional and confident. There are cautions, though.

- Keep your pockets empty so you don't jingle change or keys

- Use just one pocket at a time

- Don't over-use your pockets—it can look like a nervous habit

The dreaded casualness my teacher warned us of, today makes a speaker look and feel confident.

Voice—A speaker's voice is critical to his or her success. There are several things you can do to keep your voice "in tune."

▸ *No dairy products*—Many people have allergic reactions to dairy products. This can cause the voice to sound raspy and coarse due to the build up of phlegm. A day before a major presentation, eliminate dairy from your diet: milk, cream, butter, ice cream, yogurt, cheese, cottage cheese, etc.

▸ *Vocal warm ups*—The vocal cords are made up of bands of striated muscle, just like your thighs and biceps. When you go jogging you stretch out your leg muscles. By the same token, your voice will sound better for that early morning presentation if you warm it up. On the way to your talk, sing along to your favorite album. Also do vocal warm-ups by singing notes from as high up in your vocal range as you can go, to as low as you can go.

▸ *Stay lubricated*—If you do speaking for any length of time, i.e., half-day or full-day seminars, we recommend Ricola mints. These are herbal, non-medicated throat lozenges that will keep your throat moist and your voice sounding smooth.

Pause—The pause is the "invisible" skill. All the other style hierarchy skills are things that you *do*. The pause is what you *don't do*—that is, you stop speaking. It is the hardest of the skills to master, yet it is one of the most potent. A speaker who can pause . . . can captivate any audience.

When the speaker pauses, the audience pays closer attention. The speaker must then be ready for that attention and not embarrassed by it, as many novice speakers are. By pausing you will focus the audience's attention. You will also increase their retention of your content.

Pause as you begin your presentation and also at the end. Pause before and after critical points to imprint them in the minds of your listeners. To pause easily you will need to be very confident in your material and well rehearsed. A pause of three to four seconds is about right for effective business talks.

Use a tape recorder and a watch to try the pause with familiar material. You may be surprised how hard it is to do. You may also be surprised at how effective it is.

Eye Interaction—"Looking directly at the people in my audience when I'm speaking just sucks the thoughts right out of my head," said one workshop participant. At first, direct eye contact can be disarming for the presenter; but it may also be *the most effective* style technique a speaker can master.

Sustained eye interaction with individuals in the audience increases your credibility. It also reduces your nervousness. "What? How can that be?" you are saying.

"In high school public speaking class they told me to look at a spot on the back wall and *not* to look at people—that would make me too nervous." Most of us can talk one-on-one easily, but put 30 or 300 people in the room and we get scared. So the trick is to pick out individuals in your audience, randomly around the room and have short one-on-one conversations.

Speakers with impact tend to focus on *individuals* in the audience as they deliver key points. They stay with one person for a complete thought. Then their eye contact may shift naturally and smoothly as they transition to their next main idea.

To learn how to stay focused on one person at a time as you deliver these critical points, rehearse your talk with a group of associates. As you learn to focus on people longer, ask for feedback. Have people raise their hands as they hear a key point delivered by you without looking away. This will help train you to do it consistently. They will report feeling more connected to you and your message. Eye interaction will then become one of your most powerful skills as a speaker.

Summary

As you master the skills of style, you will watch your confidence soar. More importantly, your audiences will pay closer attention and will retain more of what you say.

Oh, one more thing. Remember to smile—when appropriate. Your topic may be serious, but there's no reason why you can't look pleasant as you present it.

In the rest of this section you will find pieces on body language, controlling nervousness, preparation, characterization, dress and voice.

The Snooze Factor: How to Beat It

Ever been so bored or distracted by a speaker that you would give *anything* to stretch out for a little siesta? Or have you found yourself glancing at your watch every thirty seconds and wondering why the time is passing so slowly?

Have you noticed that often, these snooze-masters are high-level executives or technical gurus who should have long since developed better presentation skills? We have all suffered through such presentations and perhaps, just perhaps, we have been that kind of presenter at one time ourselves.

Boring presentations in business are costly in at least three ways:

- ► They hurt the presenter's career.

- ► The audience's time is wasted.

- ► The audience fails to get the message.

Two Communication Errors

Speakers can miss the mark for two reasons. First, boring speakers do not communicate *enthusiasm*. They lack energy, excitement and power. In an attempt to establish credibility they become too academic and factual. Their talks are too detail-oriented to hold people's attention. While they may feel enthusiastic inside, what the audience experiences is the monotone voice, the lack of gestures and no eye interaction

Second, a speaker can have plenty of energy, yet demonstrate distracting visual or vocal mannerisms so severe that the audience simply is unable to pay attention to the content.

I recently heard a world-renowned authority on human brain function. I had been looking forward to the presentation with great anticipation. As he got rolling, though, he began to pace and speak in a rhythmic monotone. I glanced around the audience and saw many people with glazed eyes. His repetitive, distracting mannerisms actually put people into a light hypnotic trance.

Vocal mannerisms such as odd rhythm, a monotone voice, use of phrases and non-words like "you know," "uh" and long-winded sentences, create communication blocks for the audience.

Repetitive, unconscious, nervous gestures not only distract an audience's attention, they communicate lack of confidence and nervousness.

Making Changes

Sigmund Freud, the father of psychoanalysis, once said that dreams are "the royal road to the unconscious." Similarly, in presentation skills training, video is the "royal road to the unconscious." We become aware of our unconscious habit patterns by seeing ourselves doing them. This is the first step to change.

It is hard to be aware of our "style" and mannerisms while we speak. Video or audio tape feedback helps us to become aware of how we look and sound to our audience, which can help us eliminate annoying habits and boring delivery.

Videotape is becoming more readily available in many organizations and in presentation skills training. In our PowerSpeaking® programs, people see their tapes, analyze their style and make immediate changes.

Even more powerful than video, though, is "stop-action coaching." This involves stopping a speaker as he or she is doing something that needs to be corrected (or reinforced). In this way, the speaker can incorporate changes during the presentation and start learning immediately the new, more effective style of delivery. To do this, get together a small audience, i.e., friends, colleagues or family—and ask them to make suggestions *as you deliver your talk*. While this will be disorienting at first, the long-term payoff in improving your style will be worth it.

Of Liars and Speakers

Tentatively, Susan approached the lectern. Then she stumbled through a talk that was well-researched, but unrehearsed. She made few gestures. The ones she did make were held close to her body. Her voice sounded higher than usual, she spoke too fast and she fiddled with her hair and jewelry. Just signs of nervousness. Nothing to worry about, right? Wrong.

Susan undercut her credibility with her nervous mannerisms. In fact, her behavior at the lectern caused some people in the audience to wonder if she was lying. According to startling new research from the field of kinesthesiology—the study of human movement—Susan's delivery style reflected what people do when they are *consciously lying* to deceive the listener.

When people lie they:

- keep gestures close to the body and gesture infrequently;

- raise their vocal pitch and speak fast;

- fidget with their clothes, jewelry, hair, etc.

These are also behaviors we all exhibit when we feel nervous speaking before a group. Does the audience chalk it up to nervousness or do they unconsciously doubt what the speaker says? Confident delivery is correlated with content believability. To make sure you create no doubt in your audience's minds about your excellent content and message, work on delivery by:

- ▸ using strong, bold, "Zone II" gestures;
- ▸ lowering your pitch and using pauses;
- ▸ not fidgeting.

Absolutely essential: REHEARSE! If you are saying it out loud to the audience for the first time, they will surely pick up your nervousness. Don't give them reason to doubt. For more information on this research, read *Telling Lies* by Paul Ekman.

The Perils of Adrenalin

Contributed by Mary McGlynn

"I get scared to death."

"Total panic. It's not for the faint hearted."

"I get butterflies, sweat buckets and shake in my boots. Other than that, it's fine."

Those were some responses I got when I asked colleagues, "How do you feel when you give a speech?"

Unfortunately, the nervousness we experience at the thought of public speaking creates a response similar to being attacked: an adrenalin rush (which usually makes you feel *more* nervous). For the speaker, the key is not to *eliminate* this physiological response, but to learn how to control it and make it work for you.

Let's look at some common physical reactions to speech-making and some suggestions for turning terror into manageable excitement.

Cotton Mouth—When you combine fear with a lot of talking and nervous smiling, the end result is a dry mouth. Have a pitcher or glass of water at the lectern. Use lozenges to keep your mouth moist. (Ricola Natural Herb Cough Drops, for example.) To produce saliva, bite the side of your tongue or massage the roof of your mouth. Stay away from coffee and tea. Drink warm water.

Sweating—Have you seen *Broadcast News*? As the neophyte broadcaster does the weekend edition for the first time, sweat pours down his face in a veritable river making his credibility as soggy as his shirt.

If sweating is a problem for you, a flimsy Kleenex will not do the trick. Use a large, cloth handkerchief. For women, dress shields (from high school prom days) are still available at the local dime store.

Freezing—Think about being "scared stiff." Your muscles are rigid, your knuckles are white and your face is set in stone. You are the picture of terror. As difficult as it is to do, you can only combat the "frozen" look by forcing yourself to move. Unlock your grasp of the lectern and try a few gestures. Make a point away from the lectern. Strive for a heightened conversational style and connection with your audience through eye interaction and a feeling of passion for your message.

Note: Giving a superior speech also requires good physical balance. For women, high-heels or cramped feet will knock you off-kilter (physically *and* mentally), so wear comfortable, low-heeled shoes. (See "High-Heel Horror," pg. 78.)

High Pitch—Generally, the faster you speak, the higher your pitch. Try speaking more slowly. Pause between sentences and key points. Tape-record your speeches and listen to yourself.

Lower your pitch by sitting in a chair and placing a book on the floor in front of you. Lean over limply. Read aloud to the floor and notice the resonance in your chest. Sit up and consciously recreate that relaxed lower tone. Breathing and relaxation exercises are key to lowering your pitch.

Hoarseness—Strained, loud talking and nervous tension can create hoarseness. The throat tightens and consequently, strains the vocal cords. Be aware of your body. Relax your throat. Depend on your diaphragm for volume. *Project* your voice rather than shout. If hoarseness persists, see an ear, nose and throat specialist to rule out a medical cause; then see a speech therapist for exercises to develop proper use of your voice.

Nausea—Nausea may develop as a result of adrenalin and other attack response chemicals pumping wildly through your body. If you do feel sick, slow, deep exhalation breathing will help.

Brain Death—This is a nightmare when it happens. Often we go blank because we memorize a talk and try to recall it word-for-word. To minimize the chances of brain death, use notes. Visualize stories so that words flow easily. When you're in front of the room, pause, take a drink of water and allow your visual memory to bring back the image you had in mind through rehearsal.

Other Tips For Relaxation

In their book *Speaking Up* (McGraw Hill, 1977), Janet Stone and Jane Bachner suggest that the best way to reduce speech terror is through preparation (75%). Other ways include breathing exercises (15%), physical and mental preparation (10%).

Rehearsal—*Advance preparation is the key to developing a sense of confidence.* You know what to expect. You can connect with your audience since the content is secure in your mind. Know and choreograph the opening of your speech so that you can come on strong.

Breathing—Breathing exercises signal your body to relax. Just as you practice delivering the content of your talk, also practice relaxation breathing. Get comfortable. Focus on an object. Take a few deep breaths. Feel your body respond. Know that you can draw on that same relaxed feeling during a talk.

Physical and Mental Exercises—Try a few neck rolls. Alternate facial tensing with big, wide-mouth stretches. Also, tense and relax your whole body. Shake your legs, arms and fingers to get rid of that excess tension. Appreciate your preparation and knowledge of the topic. See in your mind the delivery of a successful speech—and then go do it.

Remember every speaker is affected by the perils of adrenalin but there are many options open to you. To turn nervous energy into focused excitement take the time for rehearsal, relaxation breathing and physical exercises. It's with that sense of control and preparedness you can turn the queasy stomach and frozen body into positive energy. That excitement can work for you.

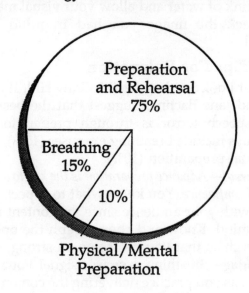

Preparation and Rehearsal 75%

Breathing 15%

10%

Physical/Mental Preparation

With a Little Help from Your Friends

The Apollo flights were off course 90% of the time—and yet they always reached the moon. It was continuous feedback, followed by corrective action by the crew that ensured the success of the missions. In speaking, too, we need feedback. Without it, it's almost impossible to know if our speech is "on course."

Some time ago I was the keynote speaker at the American Society of Military Comptrollers' annual convention in Denver. There were over 2,500 people from all around the world in attendance. I was determined to make this an excellent talk. While developing the speech, I decided to invite feedback from people who know about speaking. The idea of getting direct critiques from colleagues in a "dress rehearsal" presentation was terrifying. But the alternative of delivering an ordinary talk to such an audience was unacceptable.

That critique session was one of the most powerful learning experiences I've had as a professional speaker. To gain this advantage for your next major presentation consider doing a dress rehearsal with feedback. Some tips:

The Right People—Invite people who have experience speaking and/or who know about your topic area.

They should be people who care about your success and who work well in a group. Exclude the big egos. A good sized group is eight to ten.

Timing—Plan your rehearsal two to three weeks before your big talk. This will give you time to make content, visual aid and delivery changes as necessary.

Preparation and Rehearsal—Develop the content and visual aids well before the dress rehearsal. Even though you anticipate changes later, give your talk *out loud* five or six times (with visuals) before the dress rehearsal. Your rehearsal audience should see your talk as a finished product. Include a copy of your speech outline for them to follow along.

Setting—Book a conference or hotel room for your dress rehearsal. Duplicate as closely as possible the setting for your big talk. Block out at least twice the allotted time of your talk for the feedback.

Although you won't have to pay people for their participation, plan to take everyone to lunch or dinner after the critique session. Remember to have coffee service. This token of your appreciation also allows for more feedback.

Frequent Feedback—Build in at least three places for critique during the dress rehearsal session. Logical times might be after the main introduction, during the body of the talk and at the end. Allow at least ten minutes for each discussion period.

What's the Payoff for Them?—People who attend your rehearsal session will find it a very stimulating experience in improving their own speaking. They will be glad they gave you their time. As a final gesture of thanks, send them an audio or videotape copy of your talk. They will hear and see how you incorporated their suggestions.

The people who attended my dress rehearsal made invaluable suggestions. Most comments involved content rather than delivery. Someone even spotted a typo on one of my slides. My talk in Denver was far better than it would have been because seven people unselfishly gave of their time on a Saturday morning to give me constructive feedback.

So, whether you are preparing a major address or launching a moon shot, be sure to include feedback into the process. You will greatly improve your odds of reaching your destination.

What Speakers Can Learn from Actors

Do you want to be a more dynamic, persuasive speaker, trainer or business presenter? If so, watch show-business professionals. In fact, you may even want to take acting lessons.

"Hold on," you say. "I am a businessperson. I give business (or technical) talks to boards of directors, internal staff people or customers. Acting isn't for me! Leave that entertainment stuff to Dustin Hoffman and Meryl Streep. I have *serious* talks to deliver."

Absolutely. Your message is important. That is why it has to be delivered well. Writing in *Success Magazine*, Therese McNally (an actress and former stockbroker) said: "Every time a businessperson makes a presentation or gives a speech, he or she is indeed performing."

By intently focusing on content (facts, statistics, logic), we often lose sight of the purpose of our talk—to communicate. Television, theater and film professionals communicate for a living. They know how to hold an audience's attention. By looking to them for pointers, we can become better at getting our messages across.

Audience Contact

I recently saw a stage show starring Joel Grey. As he joked, sang and danced around the stage, he had the audience in the palm of his hand. He did it by interacting with us and by acknowledging audience responses.

Business presenters can learn from Joel. For starters, get out from behind the lectern or the overhead projector. Move around physically—even move out into the audience. Along the same line, extended eye interaction with people around the room will greatly increase your believability and rapport. Eye interaction projects confidence. It also reduces nervousness because you get the sense of talking one-on-one to individuals rather than to a sea of faces.

Finally, make your audience feel a "part of the show" by encouraging responses or dialogue about your presentation.

Speaking with the Body

When we get up to speak, we usually do "what comes naturally"—that is, unconsciously. It may not be effective. For example, walking back and forth on stage without purpose becomes nervous pacing. Constant, unconscious arm and hand movements can also be distracting.

Gestures that help paint verbal pictures in the listener's mind can be very effective. They should be thought through in advance, if not actually rehearsed. Voice range, pacing and intensity are other areas that need to be considered. Practicing these platform skills, especially with video feedback, will help the speaker to be more dynamic.

Actors work a lot with movement, gestures and voice. They become conscious of responses the rest of us are generally unconscious of. Presenters who are aware of how they use their bodies and voices are more powerful communicators.

Characterization

Outstanding presenters tell stories that enrich their presentation content. Stories give audiences emotional handles that help them grasp your meaning. Whether you are telling stories about yourself or about other people, try to become your characters. In your mind (and body), be back in the situation you are describing. The clearer you can see and feel it, the better the audience will get your message.

Acting is not pretending to be someone you are not. It is more a process of empathy with the character you are portraying.

Rehearsal

Business presenters rarely rehearse. We spend hours writing and researching our talk, but never take time to actually rehearse it *out loud*. Rehearse with an audio or video recorder, or by practicing in front of family members or the bathroom mirror. This will greatly increase your confidence and impact.

> *"The art of acting consists of keeping people from coughing."*
> —*Sir Ralph Richardson*

Stage Fright?
Change Your Face!

John is gripping the lectern so tightly his knuckles are turning white. His voice is breathy and weak. His face is frozen with the look of terror: eyes wide, eyebrows up in the middle, lips thin and tense. Could it be that John is *increasing* his own fear through his face and body? Traditional wisdom and modern science say yes.

Around 1900 the great American psychologist William James suggested that bodily reactions create emotional reality, i.e., my body is stiff, therefore I'm afraid. Recent studies support this view. In the field of psychophysiology researchers are finding that by changing our facial expressions, we can change our inner physiology and hence, our emotions. By altering facial muscles, people can recreate the physiological reactions of fear, anger, disgust, sadness, happiness and surprise. Investigators correlate changes in certain autonomic nervous system measures like: heart rate, skin conductivity, finger temperature and respiration rate with facial configurations. Writing in the journal, *Psychophysiology*, psychologist Paul Ekman summarized the findings of a recent study: "Results indicated that voluntary facial activity produced significant levels of subjective experience of the associated emotion."

What does all of this mean to John as he shakes and quakes at the lectern? His facial expression of fear is probably reinforcing the inner bodily sensation of fear. To begin feeling more relaxed, John needs to change his face. By smiling, using his eyebrows and relaxing his mouth, John can create the inner feelings of relaxed confidence. And so can all speakers. To start *feeling* relaxed, all we have to do is start *looking* relaxed.

> *"Action seems to follow feeling, but really action and feeling go together; and by regulating the action, which is under the more direct control of the will, we can indirectly regulate the feeling, which is not."*
>
> —William James
> *Psychologist*

The Sound of Your Voice

Contributed by Carol Fleming, Ph.D.

The Secrets We Tell!

With the sound of your voice, you are sending out a constant stream of signals about what is going on inside—your feelings, thoughts and attitudes, as well as indications of personality, social status, education and intelligence. People are expert receivers and analyzers of these signals. Are you sending the right message?

Are you inadvertently telling your listener that you are not sure of yourself or that you don't have the educational background to handle the job all because of the way you use your voice or pronounce your words? Unfortunately, people usually will not point this out to you because it is rude and difficult to do. Rather, they just won't give you the business. So how, then, can you learn how you really sound to others? It is not as hard as you might think, but it does take courage.

A Difficult Challenge

The average person has a terrible aversion to the sound of his or her own voice. There are several reasons for this. When we speak, all we know is our own internal meaning. (We can only guess about what the impact is on our listeners.) All of our mental circuitry is involved in the speaking process and we simply don't have the ability to observe ourselves objectively at the same time.

What You Can Do

Evaluating other people's voices, as well as your own, is the first step to understanding what unconscious voice patterns are. Here are some ways you can get the insight you need.

Tape Recorder—Using a quality tape recorder, record people talking in normal conversation. As you listen, ignore the content of what they say, but focus on how they say it. Listen for pitch levels, speed, interruptions, quantity of speech, loudness, etc. You will become increasingly aware of how these features influence your opinion of others.

Modeling—Identify the speech patterns and voice qualities that you admire. It helps to have a model, for example, a radio or television broadcaster. First, *listen* to (but don't watch) the speaker. Then, turn down the volume and just *watch* the speaker. Notice the movement of the lips and how many of the speaker's teeth are visible. (People who mumble don't move their jaws or lips much and don't show their teeth when they speak.)

Record and Listen—Record yourself as you talk informally on the phone to a friend. Then, listen for your unconscious speech patterns on the tape. Awareness of these patterns is an essential part of the change process.

When we hear ourselves on tape, we may feel totally alien to the voice. You may think to yourself: "It doesn't feel like my internal 'me' at all." Remember those "expert analyzer" abilities we all have? Suddenly you are using them to focus on you. The tape recorder can make you become very self-conscious, but be careful not to be hypercritical.

Remember, we are constantly being evaluated by others by how we speak and use our voices. Like any learned behavior, voice quality can be changed. Make yours the best it can be.

> *"The devil hath not in all his quiver's choice,*
> *an arrow for the heart like a sweet voice."*
> —Lord Byron

Practice Makes ~~Perfect~~ Better

Contributed by Talya Bauer

Have you ever wondered why some people can get up in front of a large audience and give a brilliant speech while others do fine going over their talk alone but "bomb" in front of an audience? The answer is simple—practice! Practice plays a vital role in whether the presence of an audience will lead to a spectacular presentation or a poor one.

In the early 1900s, E. Meumann, an exercise researcher, discovered the amazing effect of audience presence on performance. In front of others, his subjects lifted more weight than they ever could alone! At first researchers thought that doing tasks in front of an audience lead directly to enhanced performance. But over the years the research results were conflicting. Sometimes the presence of an audience helped to enhance performance and sometimes performance was hampered.

Light was shed on this paradox in the 1960s when Robert B. Zajonc presented his theory that helped to explain these conflicting results. His explanation involved "dominant responses." When a set of behaviors are simple or well-learned, they become dominant responses. When complex tasks are attempted under stressful conditions, like giving a presentation in front of an audience, people are likely to revert to their dominant responses.

What does this mean for you if you have a talk to give in two weeks? It means that practice is vital to your success. The mere presence of one other person raises anxiety or arousal levels by touching off basic alertness responses. In other words—we get nervous. When nervousness sets in, our reactions become more automatic (dominant response) and we are in danger of reverting back to bad habits like pacing, avoiding eye contact or nervous fidgeting.

Even though we may know better, without practice, the most effective responses may allude us. While this may sound frightening, it doesn't have to be. Now that you know about rehearsal you can use the audience to your benefit. Studies show that overlearning or over-practicing are essential in maintaining desired performance during periods of emergency and stress. The more you've rehearsed your presentation skills and material, the more your dominant response will be to give a spectacular talk!

Dress and Appearance

Just as inappropriate gestures can detract from a speaker's substance, the dress and appearance of a speaker can do the same. On the day of your big presentation dress appropriately for the audience and occasion. Dress comfortably so that you can move freely across the stage. Wear darker, solid colors for greater authority and be sure your clothes are well-tailored. Here are some more specific tips:

Tips for Women

- ▶ Wear a jacket for credibility.
- ▶ Wear business appropriate neckline and hem.
- ▶ Gain stability by wearing lower heeled shoes with closed back and toe or flats.
- ▶ Wear natural or subtle colored hose.
- ▶ Keep hair soft, controlled and away from face.
- ▶ Avoid distracting, noisy jewelry.
- ▶ Wear a tasteful amount of makeup.

Tips for Men

- ▶ Take everything out of pockets!
- ▶ Wear ties to belt-buckle length.
- ▶ Generally use a four-in-hand (small) tie knot.

► Pay attention to the length of sleeves and cuffs.

► Have a slight break in the length of slacks/suit pants.

By paying attention to your dress and appearance, you will eliminate the risk of distractions that may reduce the impact of your message. Be aware of this critical aspect of your style and you will increase the overall impact of your presentation.

High-Heel Horror

Contributed by Mary McGlynn

"Strong, stable presentation. Direct and to the point. I applaud you." Little did the evaluator know that he had also witnessed a revolutionary act. Before the talk, I had dumped my high-heels. Sensible, flat shoes forever!

For too long women have set themselves up for speaking failure by dressing poorly. Wobbly, nervous legs perched on high-heels inevitably take our minds off the solid content of any presentation.

Every day, women walk into presentations with a disadvantage. When the normal amount of nervousness is coupled with two- or three-inch heels, we have a disaster waiting to happen. It does not have to be that way.

Wearing high-heeled shoes is often expected in business settings. We hear comments like: "It's businesslike," or "Heels look appropriate with my business suits," or "They make me feel taller." According to Susan Brownmiller in her 1984 book, *Femininity*, the issue of femininity is also paramount to understanding our drive for the sleek heel. She says that high-heels:

  ► make the foot look smaller;

▸ are usually light and flimsy in construction;

▸ limit freedom of movement as the physical energy is redirected to maintaining balance;

▸ reverse the functional reason why we originally chose to wear shoes;

▸ create a sex difference that impedes our ability to walk;

▸ are a hindrance that no man in his right mind would tolerate.

Times have changed. Today we have a choice. No longer are we stuck with two choices: very high-heels or very ugly, "practical" shoes. Flats are everywhere. They are sleek and professional. They are appropriate for business and casual attire.

For your next presentation, consider the benefits of flat shoes:

▸ They offer stability so that you can concentrate on your message.

▸ Even though the adrenalin may be pumping, you can count on your feet as a strong, anchored base.

▸ Movement to make a point or to get closer to your audience is done with greater ease and more fluid, graceful motion.

▸ Just as rehearsal gives you greater control of the content, the decision to wear flats will give you greater control of your body.

As one buyer for a larger shoe store put it: "The majority of women have gotten some sense. Comfort is critical. There are now decent-looking flats. Now a woman can have style and comfort." Professional women are turning their backs on the very high-heel.

Suggestions for buying shoes include: buy leather, buy quality, buy comfort, work with a salesperson that knows how to fit your foot and knows the product line.

The buyers we talked to recommended brand names: Joyce-Selby, Cole-Hahn, Amalfi, Evans, Bali, Farragamo, Nordstrom, Palomo, Via Spiga, Bandolino, Caressa, Nickels. Rockport and SAS for casual.

For your next presentation try wearing lower-heeled shoes. Your comfort and balance are too important to be taken lightly.

The Staging of Speaking

> Elephants don't bite; it's the gnats and mosquitoes that get you.
>
> Joel Weldon
> Professional Speaker

The content and the delivery can be world-class but if the staging is ignored, the presentation can bomb. Staging is often overlooked, yet it is critical. This chapter covers the two aspects of good staging: the environment and the people.

Environmental concerns are things like: equipment, lighting, temperature, visual aids and sound. People issues involve: disruptive behavior, question-and-answer sessions, audience participation and panel discussions. All of these are covered in this chapter.

Working with Hotels: Advice from the Experts

Contributed by Mary McGlynn

When you are giving a talk and it's not on your turf, what can you do to ensure success? To find out we went to two recognized experts. John Parke is the director of marketing at the San Francisco Airport Marriott and Carlos Gonzalez is the banquet manager from the Garden Court Hotel in Palo Alto.

John and Carlos say the same thing: If you want everything to go smoothly, be sure to do three things:

Communicate your needs well in advance. This is no time to be secretive or last minute. Tell your meeting planner everything so nothing is left to chance. What are your AV requirements? How do you want the tables and room configured? Will you need any last-minute technical support services? What about lighting?

Put everything in writing. When information is written, fewer interpretation problems crop up. John estimates that 95% of all problems develop because erroneous assumptions are made or oral instructions are forgotten or misinterpreted. Send your room diagram ahead, complete with dimensions. List all the required equipment. Explain your microphone needs.

Get agreement on what you, the meeting planner and the hotel staff are each responsible for. Leave nothing to chance.

Arrive early! Last-minute, late-arrival speakers create ulcers for themselves and for the hotel staff. By getting there early you will have time for positive interactions with the hotel staff well in advance of your presentation.

When you are comfortable, the speech or seminar is more likely to go well. Check everything in the room. Use the microphone. Check the room arrangement. Know who to call in the event of a problem and get familiar with the person in charge. Once you feel comfortable with everything, take a walk so you can mentally and physically prepare for a dynamic presentation.

What about the intense time about half an hour before the presentation? John suggests you keep calm—and talk to the right person. Problems are often created because of unexpected last-minute requirements. Don't tell the AV technician and the banquet staff and the waiters of a last-minute change. Talk to the convention service manager. S/he can get the problem solved almost immediately.

A smile, a little humor and a "thank you" go a long way during those tense few minutes before the presentation, according to Carlos. The Golden Rule (treat others the way you would like to be treated) gets golden results. Carlos gives an example from personal experience. "Last week when Mr. Gilbert came to do his seminar at the Garden Court, I came in on my time off because I knew a building across the street from the hotel was going to be torn down that day. I also knew the seminar room he had chosen was going to be very noisy. Within a matter of minutes we rearranged the location of the seminar, we adjusted the design of the room and we were ready before the first participant walked in. Mr. Gilbert really thanked me. I felt good about my job. I felt I made a difference."

One last piece of advice comes from John. Be sure to tell the hotel *everything* so there are no surprises. An example he cites occurred when three different groups were running individual seminars in the same logistical area of the hotel. Suddenly a marching band appeared as part of an opening ceremony for one of the groups. Had the hotel staff known about the marching band, alternative arrangements could have been made for the two other seminars. "With clear communication everyone wins: the speaker, the meeting planner and the hotel."

So the next time you are speaking away from the office, take the advice of experts: communicate effectively well in advance, get to know the hotel staff member who can solve your problems and put everything in writing. When you heed the advice of John and Carlos, success will be yours on any turf.

Staging with E's

Speaking and training programs often require miscellaneous audio-visual support items. The lack of these little things can torpedo your program. Don't let the "gnats and mosquitoes" get you. Use this list to check that you have taken care of everything ahead of time.

Equipment, Essentials, Environment

Equipment	*Needed*
Flip Chart/Pads	_____
Overhead Projector	_____
Screen	_____
35mm Slide Projector/Bulb	_____
Projector Table	_____
VCR Playback Unit (size: _____)	_____
TV Monitor	_____
Jacks (miscellaneous)	_____
Microphone	_____
Hand-held _____	
Clip-on _____	
Wireless _____	
Lectern/Podium	_____
Tape Recorder	_____
Chalkboard	_____
Videotapes	_____
Audio tapes	_____

Essentials	_Needed_
Adapters	_____
Chalk	_____
Eraser	_____
Extension Cord	_____
Marking Pens	
(flip chart, white board)	_____
Paper	_____
Pencils	_____
Pointer	_____
Scissors	_____
Screwdriver	_____
Tape (masking, gaffers)	_____
Tweezers (for jammed slides)	_____
White-Out	_____
_____	_____
_____	_____
_____	_____
_____	_____

Environment

Seating Arrangement (attach a diagram)

   ❏ Theater   ❏ Conference   ❏ Herringbone

   ❏ Classroom   ❏ Horseshoe   ❏ Rounds

Dimension of Room _____

Location of controls:

     Heating _____
     Lighting _____
     Ventilation _____
     PA System _____

Location of:

     Rest Rooms _____
     Telephones _____

A Speaker's Nightmare: The Out-Of-Control Audience

It was the first day of a week-long conference for a small, strife-ridden, high-tech company. The day's meetings had ended at 4:00 PM and people adjourned to the bar. Then there was a "social hour" from 6:00-7:00. Afterwards, four different kinds of wine were served with dinner. The audience was loud and boisterous. In fact, they were roaring drunk. It was 8:45 PM—after a long dinner. And I was the "motivational" speaker.

By the time I came on, the group was hurling insults at each other, at their competition—and at me. It was just short of a food fight. What did I do? Opened with my serious, thought-provoking Oliver Wendell Holmes quote, of course. One of the ring-leaders at the back of the room slid down in his chair, rolled his eyes skyward and let out a loud groan. It went downhill from there.

How does a presenter control disruptive audience behavior? What would you have done?

While most speakers *rarely* have to deal with such outrageous audience behavior, you can expect minor disruptions often. Be aware that:

- ► You do not have to put up with rude audience behavior.
- ► Your audience wants you to take charge of inappropriate and disruptive individuals.
- ► You can use a series of graduated responses to gain control.

The graph shows how the intensity of your responses should increase as the disruption gets worse.

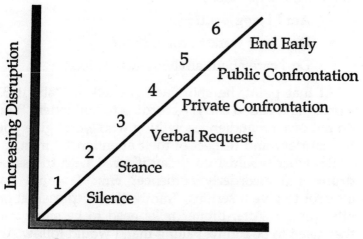

Intensity of Presenter's Response

Let's take the example of people talking during your presentation. Your increasingly stronger responses might look like this:

1) Stop talking. The unexpected silence from the front of the room will almost always bring attention back to you.

2) Walk over and stand physically near the talkers.

3) Set up small-group activities and ask the talkers to be quiet.

4) Confront the disruptive people privately during a break and enlist their cooperation.

5) Confront them publicly during the program and ask them to stop or to leave.

6) End the program early.

Remember, you always have the final option of ending early if things get too far out of control. Even pros use this strategy. When Art Linkletter recently faced a drunk and indifferent audience, he asked himself three questions:

▸ Am I being paid?

▸ Do I ever want to come back?

▸ Do I care about anybody here? No.

At that point, he shortened his talk to "about 35 words" and ended early. According to Linkletter, "You do not owe an audience anything who won't give you the courtesy and respect of their attention." Amen.

So, what would I do today if faced with the same drunk and disorderly audience? First, I would not attempt to give a serious, "motivational" presentation after dinner. After-dinner talks need to be short and they need to be funny. Failing that, I would follow Art Linkletter's advice and end early.

Remember the next time you face disruptions in an audience—be it a speech, a training program or a staff presentation—don't let them spoil the show. You have a wide range of strategies for dealing with out-of-control audiences. These tactics will keep you in control. Your audience will applaud you for it and you'll be one step closer to a more confident attitude toward speaking—even in the worst of conditions.

Dealing with
Hostile Questions

Imagine this situation: you have just completed the most important presentation of your career to a large and responsive audience. You put in weeks of preparation. Your visuals were excellent, your delivery flawless and the audience (including important decision-makers) loved it.

After the applause dies down, you ask if there are any questions. Suddenly, a hand shoots up and you hear an angry voice say: "Well, that may be all well and good, but it hardly matters when your projects are consistently late and over budget!" A hush falls on the crowd and all eyes are on you. How do you handle it?

First, Deal with Feelings—To put the angry questioner at ease and to increase your credibility in the eyes of the audience, you must acknowledge the questioner's feelings. To do this, paraphrase—that is, say in your own words—what you believe the person is feeling. Do this nonjudgmentally, reflecting the vocal tone and body language of the questioner. The purpose here is to let the person know that you understand his or her concern. Note: your response does not show agreement . . . only acknowledgment.

If you state the concern accurately, the questioner usually will nod his or her head in agreement with your restatement. This is your goal. The head-nodding often will be accompanied by a noticeable physical relaxation, because the person now knows you have heard his or her concern.

Next, Deal with Facts—Only after you have shown that you really understand his or her *emotional* position will the questioner be able to hear the logic of your response. Too often we jump right in with a logical answer or argument to an emotional statement. All this does is further antagonize the questioner.

Then, Answer Whole Group—Once you have agreement from the questioner that you really understand both the content and the feeling of the question, turn physically and move toward the whole audience.

Make the question everyone's concern. Avoid setting up a one-on-one dialogue with the questioner. And don't make eye contact with him or her as you finish your answer. This way, you will not look to the questioner for approval. Asking for approval can trigger a second or third follow-up question. Your intent should be to move on quickly to other questions.

Here's What It Sounds Like

Using the original hostile question, the following is an example of the process we just described.

Questioner (frowning): "Well that may be all well and good, but it hardly matters when your projects are late and over budget!"

You (with feeling): "Sounds like you are irritated that I painted a rosy picture in my speech when our projects are late and over budget. Is that what you mean?"

Questioner (nodding and relaxing a bit): "Yes."

You (turning away from the questioner and addressing the whole audience): "This is an important issue. Early in the year when our strategic objectives were still in flux, yes, we did miss some deadlines and were 5%

over targets. In the past nine months, though, we have been on schedule with high-quality products at, or under budget. Our future performance will be as consistent. Next question (looking away from questioner into the audience)?"

The audience silently applauds your masterful skill.

This process will help you handle difficult questions. Your response will show your respect for differing viewpoints and it will demonstrate your lack of defensiveness. The effect will be increased audience participation. Now you are ready to face any audience.

Q & A Strategies

Your speech is over. Now the hard part starts: the question-and-answer period. This is when you have the special challenge of looking confident and prepared, even though you don't know what's coming next. Here are some tips to make it go well.

Style—Remember to maintain your solid delivery style: stance, excellent eye interaction, bold gestures, etc.

Keep answers short—Q&A is a time for audience input and participation. Short answers allow more people to participate.

Anticipate questions—Advanced planning will help. Even prepare extra visuals you could use during Q&A if necessary—but not in the body of the talk.

Repeat the question—This helps if you have a large audience or when your session is being taped.

No questions—Be sure to wait; it may take a while. Also, you may "prime the pump" by asking your own question.

Too few questions—If you run out of questions before you run out of time, wrap up. Audiences rarely get mad when a speaker ends early.

Argumentative or tangential questions—Politely let the questioner know that you appreciate his/her point and can meet after the session to talk further. Then take the next question.

Don't know the answer—Admit it and volunteer to research the answer and get back to them. You may also ask if anyone in the audience knows the answer.

Timing—Include Q&A time in the total time you have. Don't let your Q&A run into someone else's time.

Don't end with questions—After the last question, have a memorable close. This can be a well-delivered story, quotation or humorous bit that reiterates your core message and wraps things up on your own terms.

Keep these strategies in mind and your next Q&A session will add value to your overall presentation.

How to Moderate a Panel Discussion

John:	"This has got to be the most boring panel I've ever heard."
Bill:	"That first speaker went on for 15 minutes. Why didn't somebody stop him?"
John:	"And you can't hear them. They all seem to be afraid of the microphone."
Bill:	"Why doesn't the moderator take charge? What a wimp."
John:	"I'd rather be out shooting a game of golf. That would be a better use of my time."
Bill:	"You got that right. Let's go."

Both exit noisily through rear door.

The panel discussion can be a powerful presentation format. It also can be a disaster if poorly managed. If you are invited to organize and/or moderate a panel, what can you do to ensure success? Here are some tips.

Panel Members—Obviously you want to choose people who have something to say. But it is equally important that you avoid people who are self-centered egomaniacs. The panel discussion is a team event. Invite people who are good team players. As much as possible select panel members to reflect audience demographics, i.e., gender, ethnicity, age, income levels, etc.

Timing—If you have a high need to be liked by everyone, forget being a panel moderator. An effective moderator is a bit like a traffic cop. Your first responsibility is to your audience. Your job is to keep the panel members within their time limits.

When inviting people to join your panel, let them know very clearly and directly what the limits are on their presentations. Also, let them know that you will *verbally interrupt them and stop them* if they exceed their time limits.

Physical Setup—Since panel members will be seated, always request a podium (raised platform) or a stage so they can be seen by the audience. You may have people seated at a table or just seated in a semicircle. In either case, the best position for the moderator is in the middle. This gives you greater visual contact with all the panel members and also gives you a strong position from which to control the flow.

Microphones can be a real pitfall for a panel. Panel members are most often not professional speakers, and usually they're intimidated by a mic. And if panelists don't use the mic they won't be heard—which means the audience will become bored. (That's when John and Bill decide to spend the afternoon on the golf links.)

Make sure you have at least one microphone per two panel members. Show panelists how to use it in advance. Encourage them to move it closer or take it in hand each time they speak. If they forget, *stop them in their presentation to remind them*. The audience will thank you for it.

Audience Participation—A great way to cap off your panel discussion is to allow time for the audience to get involved. The audience may address questions to the panel as a whole or to individual members. If it's a smaller audience with no mic, make sure you repeat the question so all can hear. With a larger group, provide a mic for audience participation.

Your Role—Remember the traffic cop image. It's your job to keep everyone within the time constraints. You also need to remain neutral in terms of the content. Encourage panel members to have a big finish to wrap up—and to keep it short.

As you finish, thank the audience for their attention and participation. Then with great enthusiasm, thank each panel member and encourage the audience to give them a strong round of applause.

If you follow these simple but essential tips, your panel will be a great success. Who knows, you may be able to keep John and Bill in their chairs rather than on the first tee!

The Athenian Myth

Do you remember in high school, a group of super-popular kids who seemed to have it made? They were socially advanced. They knew about drinking, smoking and having sex way before everyone else. They wore the right clothes and had the right friends. In a word, they were cool. And you and I were not. Or so we thought.

Most people wanted acceptance from this group. Approval from them made you feel great. Disapproval could wipe you out for days. Does all this sound familiar? In my high school the males of this group belonged to a club called "the Athenians." They wore black jackets. They could put you down with a scornful look. Performers of all kinds—but especially speakers—were very vulnerable to their harsh judgments.

At our 30-year high school reunion, our former school president, John Rose, was giving some welcoming comments to the 250 people attending the gala event. Sure enough, sitting there, right down front, at a large round table was a group of five Athenians—still hanging out in their clique. Still being judgmental. As John got into his welcoming speech, the Athenians started with their snide remarks. As the minutes went by, John got more and more rattled. By the end of his talk he was angry and defensive. The whole evening was tainted by this event.

For any of us who speak to groups the specter of this kind of audience reaction generates a lot of adrenalin. As I watched John sweating bullets on stage that night, it suddenly dawned on me. Five wise guys were creating overwhelming anxiety for John while 245 other people in the room were having a great time and enjoying John's remarks.

Bill Cosby once commented that in every audience there will be a person he nicknamed "the face." He sits there, arms folded, pouting, full of condemnation. Cosby used to play right to that person in an attempt to win him over. Now he just ignores these people and instead plays to the rest of the audience who are enjoying themselves.

Every time I see those people in my audience, I try to remember the high school reunion. I say to myself, "Hey, let 'em eat cake. Everyone else is having fun. I'll just focus on the rest of the appreciative audience." So the next time you see those Athenians in your audience, remember the other 99% who think you're great. There is life after high school.

Audience Satisfaction

The current business buzzword is "customer satisfaction." Likewise, to be successful speakers, we must have "audience satisfaction" as our goal.

The key to satisfying your audience is to give them a presentation that:

- ▸ is tight and well organized;
- ▸ is delivered with enthusiasm;
- ▸ involves them.

We asked a cross-section of our business audiences: "What is wrong with business presentations today?" The picture that emerged from over 250 responses could not have been more emphatic.

Business and technical audiences are tired of speakers who use too many overhead slides, include too much detail and are poorly organized. Boring delivery or reading a talk also puts off audiences. Poor audience control or no audience interaction is also irritating.

Specifically, the responses fell into these three categories:

SUBSTANCE
  Poor organization
  Too much detail
	33%

STYLE
  Monotone, boring delivery
  Reading overhead slides
  No gestures, movement, eye contact
	44%

STAGING
  Too many overhead slides
  No audience interaction
  Poor audience control
	18%

Presentations delivered "on the fly" will gain few points. Too much minutiae will not work either. One person identified the problem as *an overemphasis on the importance of the detail.*

The old Sergeant Joe Friday approach ("Just the facts, Ma'am"), is simply too boring for today's audiences conditioned by the fast pace of television. Audiences are not content to sit passively and be talked at. They want to participate.

The survey information makes it clear what audiences *don't* want from a speaker. What can you do, then, to guarantee you'll be an audience-pleaser next time you take to the podium?

Substance—Have a clear core message. Keep it short and to the point. Save the detailed supportive information for the handouts. State your conclusion or point of view early in the talk and again at the end. Keep in mind that people remember longest what they hear first and what they hear last. Provide an action step, what is expected from the talk.

Style—Make it big, bold and purposeful. Remember, being effective "on stage" requires a bigger presence than talking one-on-one. Build into your presentation schedule time to rehearse. It's almost impossible to have a powerful delivery style when you are doing it for the first time. Rehearsal, to be of value, has to include standing up, moving around and delivering the talk *out loud*.

"Thinking about it" is not rehearsal. If possible, practice in front of other people. Work on all the style skills: stance, movement, gestures, voice, pause and eye interaction. Practice with your visual aids.

Staging—Include the audience. Ask them relevant questions and get a show of hands. If appropriate, have a question and answer session. Keep your answers short to include as many people as time allows.

As a speaker, your audience is your customer. You wouldn't sell your customer a defective product. Similarly, since you know what audiences want, it's now possible to give them a "zero defects" presentation.

Business presentations are just too important to your company and to your career to take casually. Put in that extra time. You will soon become known as a speaker who knows how to satisfy an audience.

Listening to Your Audience

Contributed by Diana Bonet

As speakers, we don't think of ourselves as listeners. We assume that we talk and the audience listens. Such assumptions are generally true, but there is more to it than that. Successful speakers understand the power of audience feedback through verbal and nonverbal messages.

We listen to audience feedback for two reasons:

► to verify that they heard what we said; and

► if we don't listen to them, they won't listen to us.

How to Listen to Verbal Feedback

Encourage Audience Participation—To encourage trust and build rapport, get the audience to interact with you. Ask questions, take a poll or do a survey. When someone asks a question, look directly at the person and pay close attention to what s/he is saying. Lean forward, nod in agreement, look interested. Make sure your own nonverbal feedback shows acceptance.

Acknowledge the Audience—People want to be recognized. The way we, as speakers, respond makes a difference. Treat all comments and questions with respect and thank audience members for their participation.

Be careful not to start formulating your answer to someone while the person is speaking. Give the person your undivided attention. Repeat what they said for clarity, pause a moment to think, then answer. You can give a C+ answer without thinking, but you can give an A+ answer if you pause to organize and frame your response.

Repeat What You Hear—Take the time to paraphrase or repeat a question word-for-word. Try to pick up the feelings in the question and feed that back as well, especially if the question is challenging or hostile:

Q. "How can you justify these prices?"
A. "You feel our prices are too high?"

Repeat the question for your own understanding and for the benefit of others in the audience who may not have heard it. If you are taping your speech, be sure to repeat the question for the tape.

How to Listen to Nonverbal Feedback

Watch Your Audience—To gauge an audience's response, look for signs of restlessness or dissent—heads rotating side-to-side, rigid body posture, folded arms across the chest, rolling or narrowing eyes, scowling. Develop sensitivity to this feedback. Be aware that the audience can affect you positively or negatively with its nonverbal behavior.

Make Eye Contact—See your audience as individuals. Establish eye contact with as many people as possible in different parts of the room. Eye contact is the speaker's best nonverbal tool for connecting with the audience and getting their feedback.

Pay Attention to Non-word Signals—Listen for restlessness, coughing, talking, or shuffling. These nonverbal behaviors may be a sign of boredom. Tell a story, add humor, change your volume or your rate of speech.

Good speakers pay close attention to their audiences. They care about audience participation and in building trust and gaining rapport. As a speaker, put yourself in your audience's shoes. Would *you* want to listen to you?

The Power of Speaking

> "My physicist brother says 'Give me a lever and a place to stand and I'll move the world.' I say to him, 'I'll do something even tougher. Give me 1,000 words and I'll change an attitude' "
> —*Kristin Clark*
> *Hewlett-Packard*

Ultimately, your purpose in developing your speaking skill is to impact people and effect the way things turn out. This chapter presents ways to maximize your impact with any audience. We also look at the strategies of three great speakers: Abraham Lincoln (at Gettysburg), General Norman Schwarzkopf and Tom Peters.

From the Trenches to the Podium— What Speakers Can Learn from the General

After the Gulf War, General Norman Schwarzkopf, Commander of the Allied Forces, became a folk hero in great demand. Why? First, military expertise. Second, communication expertise.

What can speakers learn from the general's success? Plenty. His style was powerful and natural, his content engaging and his character irresistible. Let's look at each in more detail.

Style—Schwarzkopf used his whole body to communicate his message in a way that enhanced his credibility and his likability. In briefing sessions, he stood beside the lectern and used strong gestures. His voice, pitch and rate of delivery were varied. Eye interaction with the audience was direct. Most of all, his face was very expressive as he covered wide-ranging topics from military strategy to sympathy for the families of those killed in the line of duty.

Content—While his style was essential to his media success, it was the general's content that took him beyond the ordinary. His briefings were marked by plain talk rather than jargon and acronyms. It was obvious that he knew the numbers and the detail and could get technical when necessary, but he kept the language clear and direct for the media.

His presentations focused not on his own accomplishments but on the work of others—either U.S. or allied troops. His presentations were rich with analogies, like when he compared troop movements to the "Hail Mary" play in football. To make key points he often used the "Rule of Three":

> "There are a lot of people who are still saying that the objective of the United States was to capture Iraq and cause the downfall of the entire country. (Pause) Ladies and gentlemen, when we were here (points to map) we were 150 miles from Baghdad and there was nobody between us and Baghdad. *If it had been our intention* to take Iraq, *if it had been our intention* to destroy the country, *if it had been our intention* to overrun the country, we could have done it unopposed from this position. But that was not our intention."

Humor is another way the general captivated his audiences. When asked by a reporter: "What are your impressions of Saddam Hussein as a military strategist?" he replied, "He is not a strategist, nor is he schooled in the operational arts, nor is he a tactician, nor is he a general, nor is he a soldier. Other than that, he is a great military man."

Character—Norman Schwarzkopf's successful content and style are built on the foundation of his character. Ultimately, it's his world view and self-esteem that made him so appealing. For example, he expressed modesty and humility when asked direct questions about his role in the success of the Desert Storm campaign. He gave credit to others. Paradoxically, when asked about the war he often responded more like a dove than like a general: "Any military man worth his salt doesn't want to go to war because he knows that going to war means killing people."

Additionally, Schwarzkopf was not authoritarian in his outlook. He was capable of seeing shades of gray. When commenting on the role of the media, he noted that the First Amendment and the public's right to know must be balanced against the possibility that the enemy will get valuable battlefield information from television, which would endanger lives and the campaign. He clearly saw both sides of the argument.

Probably the most disarming and appealing thing about the general was his vulnerability. During his interview with Barbara Walters he teared up twice, once when she inquired about his relationship to his father and again when he talked about his children. What an irresistible combination: a battle-hardened general who is a respected leader and a human being who is in touch with his feelings.

In summary, what can speakers learn from Schwarzkopf's extraordinary popularity?

- ▶ *Content:* Know the details, but speak honestly and clearly about the big picture.

- ▶ *Style:* Use a strong delivery style that is based on who you are.

- ▶ *Character:* Give credit to others, see both sides of the issue and don't hesitate to speak from emotion as well as intellect.

Speakers Tell It Like It Is

What has been your worst speaking nightmare? How did you handle it? We recently asked these questions to the readers of our PowerSpeaking® newsletter. The problems most often sighted involved:

1) the hostile audience;

2) the impromptu speech; and

3) non-English speaking audiences.

Problem—When I was suddenly asked at a conference to give an impromptu brief explanation of why massage often reduces pain in terminally ill cancer patients, to an audience full of doctors.

Solution—Knowing that some of those doctors would be skeptical and want statistics and long-term research data, I told them a story about one patient, a 14-year-old boy dying of cystic fibrosis and what happened in the family dynamics after I taught his father how to massage him. They loved it.

—Helen Campbell
Massage Therapist, San Mateo, CA

Problem—Speaking to a bunch of sales reps who had a preconceived negative attitude to the material I was presenting.

Solution—Switched to an interactive style presentation so I could listen to their concerns.

—Stephen Lencioni
Hewlett-Packard, Mountain View, CA

Problem—Speaking with a very confrontational (prospective) customer about technical issues with my V.P. of R & D present!

Solution—Tried not to panic, took a deep breath, put one hand in my pocket and gestured with the other, addressed the customer's agitated feelings as well as conveyed our technical message.

—Geoff Orth
ACS, Inc., Santa Clara, CA

Problem—Delivering someone else's presentation before an audience expecting miracles.

Solution—Rehearsed as though I had written it. Then relaxed by knowing that I know the script, the audience does not! So they won't know if I make a mistake! Worked great!

—Gerard J. Mariani
Boeing, Renton, WA

Problem—Being asked at the last minute to speak on a topic that I knew nothing about.

Solution—Tried to draw "experts" from the audience into the presentation.

—Craig W. Pampeyan
Hewlett-Packard, Sunnyvale, CA

Problem—Speaking in a foreign country to a foreign audience in a semi-hostile situation.

Solution—Went slow, attempted to win them over with factual information, anecdotes and style.

—Daniel H. Diltz
Hitachi Data Systems, Kansas City, MO

Problem—Speaking to a group of about 300 Korean engineers who didn't speak much English.

Solution—It was a technical software demo of computer graphics and fortunately pictures spoke louder than words for the most part. (Some translation also helped.)

—Scott Wolfe
Autodesk, Sausalito, CA

Problem—Speaking to Japanese businessmen through a translator. They looked down at the floor the whole time.

Solution—I'd asked about their culture beforehand and that helped me understand why they were looking at the floor.

—Debbie Sweet
Hewlett-Packard, Mountain View, CA

Problem—I remember one audience that was so dead I considered checking a few of the members for vital signs. No feedback during presentation.

Solution—I just plowed ahead as lively as I could feeding off my own internal energy resources. After the talk, the audience came to life and I received more than the usual, positive feedback. It's still one of my most puzzling situations.

—Charles Hardeman
U. S. Postal Service, Baldwin Park, CA

Problem—If it's been awhile since I've given a speech, I find I'm more anxious for perfection. In other words, if I feel rusty, I'm more afraid of the audience.

Solution—I focus on my audience's needs and take the focus off me. I practice my speeches like crazy. I only speak on topics that I have researched well and have been personally touched.

—Carolyn Kay Masters
Masters Resource Group, Tucson, AZ

Problem—I was speaking to a group of college students (about 600). The goal: get them to exceed their contributions to our organization from the previous year. Forgot what I was saying—total blank screen!

Solution—Took a breath and said, "You may not believe this but I just forgot what I was saying! Could someone refresh my memory?!" Someone did, I continued and the contribution to World University Service that year was 25% over the preceding year!

—Deborah J. Zeigler
Greenberg Zeigler Associates, Teaneck, NJ

Problem—Coping with a rock 'n roll dance in room across hall.

Solution—Stopped until management took care of delaying the "music" until we were finished.

—John A. Shults
Effective Oral Communications, Houston, TX

Problem—I had a woman in the audience who wanted to discuss one point I was making. I tried to move on to other topics without success.

Solution—I finally told her that I needed to continue but would be happy to discuss it off-line.

—Karen Lewey
Hewlett-Packard, Corvallis, OR

Problem—Delivering a one-hour presentation with a recently, surgically repaired broken leg while on codeine.

Solution—Took more codeine.

—James Aguilar
Stanford, CA

Problem—I had to give a sales presentation to a potential client in the clothes I wore on the airplane the night before when my suitcase didn't arrive.

Solution—I made a joke of having an excuse to wear comfortable shoes and went on with the presentation

—Cheryl A. Karpowicz
Ecology & Environment, San Francisco, CA

Problem—A hot room at Lone Mountain College, on a hot day, with heaters that wouldn't turnoff.

Solution—Opened all the windows, took off my jacket, invited others to do so, too . . . and kept my talk short. Q & A was held outside in the shade.

—Linda Marks
Work Options Consultant, San Francisco, CA

Problem—A bunch of drunks after a long happy hour and dinner.

Solution—I don't do after-dinner speeches any more.

—George Morrisey
The Morrisey Group, Buena Park, CA

Don't Even Think About Getting It "Right"

Tips from Tom Peters

Tom Peters is co-author of *In Search of Excellence*. He is also one of the best business speakers in the country today. His July 22, 1991 management column in the *San Jose Mercury News* offered nine suggestions for speakers. It is reprinted here with permission. © 1991 TPG Communications

We all need potent persuasive skills to rope in outside money and supporters from time to time. A knack for communicating in "public" is vitally important. Having been a 150-times-a-year, for-profit yakker, I offer this advice:

Practice Makes Better—Obvious as it sounds, too many ignore it. There are damn few natural composers, golfers or race car drivers. And there are no natural speakers—at least I've never come across any. You get better at speaking by speaking and speaking.

Join Toastmasters—Toastmasters International is the Alcoholics Anonymous of the speaking world. Its ranks include generals, pastors and politicians, plus hundreds of thousands of scared speechless engineers, accountants, supervisors and vice presidents, to name a few.

Toastmasters' "guidelines" for good speaking are a touch too rigid for my taste, but the core idea is sound: you learn to get over your stage fright by starting small and constantly practicing (see No. 1 above). Seek out a local chapter and sign up—large companies sometimes even have their own chapters.

Forget All the Conventional "Rules" But One— Frankly, most laws of speechmaking—keep your hands out of your pockets, don't say "uh," lead off with a zinger—are garbage. But there is one golden rule: stick to topics you deeply care about and don't keep your passion buttoned inside your vest. An audience's biggest turn-on is the speaker's obvious enthusiasm. That's as true for a pitch to purchase a $200,000 computer system as it is for a plea to save the environment. If you're lukewarm about the issue, forget it!

Stories, Stories, More Stories—Charts and graphs have their place and a pretty prominent one in many business presentations. Nonetheless, even an analytically inclined audience will remember one poignant comment from a survey respondent ("this company really doesn't listen to the likes of us") long after forgetting your multicolored bar chart showing the firm's "openness to ideas" at 2.62 on a seven-point, sociometrically valid scale.

For Heaven's Sake, Don't Write It Out!—If spontaneity isn't everything, it verges on it. That hardly means winging it: careful preparation spawns spontaneity. But it does mean never, ever writing it out in full. If you do, you become a slave to your exact wording and inevitably lose 75 percent of any emotional impact.

Don't Even Think About "Getting It Right"—After decades of giving speeches, from five minutes to five days (with breaks!) in length, I've yet to be satisfied with one of them. But tomorrow is another day. Forget the "this is my only chance to shine" baloney. If you're worth a darn, you'll get lots of chances to shine.

Breathe!—I'm no pro when it comes to meditation. I get flush and breathless before any speech. One answer is to close your eyes (or not) and take five or 10 deep breaths (even in front of others) before going up on stage to chair that big meeting.

Get Away from the Podium—You're probably not a stiff around the office and almost certainly not at home. Why be a stiff when you're making an important presentation? Put your notes on index cards (written in bold letters if your eyes, like mine, ain't getting younger), so you won't be nailed to the lectern. Then wander around the table, into the crowd, about the platform. Look comfortable and your audience will be more comfortable, too.

Loosen Up—You're not going to convince 'em anyway. Speeches aren't about turning archenemies into cheering supporters. Presentations are mainly opportunities to reassure those who already agree with you that you're a horse worth betting on. So try to relax and enjoy yourself, to present "excited you" as excited you—which is just what the audience wants.

Quick Tips for Speakers

Project Meltdown

True story. In the middle of an important technical presentation to a large group, the speaker was shocked to see his 35mm slide projector suddenly burst into flames. The fan stopped working and the projector overheated. The carousel with all his slides literally melted. What to do?

Almost without missing a beat, the presenter reached into his briefcase and pulled out duplicate visuals in the form of overhead transparencies. The presentation was completed in fine form.

Moral: Always have backup visuals for major presentations.

Ken Blanchard on Body Language

"If you want to become a good public speaker, watch other speakers to see how they use their bodies. For example, the good public speakers I've observed walk with their shoulders back and their heads high and use a lot of hand and arm gestures."

Ken Blanchard is the author of *"The One-Minute Manager."*

The Carl Kammerer Strategy

One of the stars of the 1959 University of the Pacific football team was a linebacker named Carl Kammerer. The big rivalry that year was with Arizona State University.

At 10:30 Friday night, before the big game with ASU, Carl walked into the stadium alone. He sat on the 50-yard line—for a long time. He visualized Saturday's game: the noise, the colors, the other players. He walked the perimeter of the stadium. He got the feel of the arena. But most of all, he visualized himself playing his best game.

As a speaker, you too can benefit from this kind of winning preparation. Get to the site of your presentation early. Become familiar with the room. See yourself giving a fabulous presentation. See the audience responding warmly. Positive visualization is one of the most effective tools you can use to give an outstanding talk.

By the way, UOP won that game and Carl Kammerer was the key factor.

An Actor's Beginnings

"I was very shy and yet when I got up before an audience, I felt comfortable. One day I addressed the whole student body and talked for about 10 minutes.

All of a sudden I was making them laugh, I was making them listen and I felt very powerful. It was an exhilarating feeling."

—Richard Widmark

> "If I went back to college again, I'd concentrate on two areas: learning to write, and to speak before an audience. Nothing in life is more important than the ability to communicate effectively."
>
> —Gerald R. Ford

Peak Performance Under Pressure

Contributed by Jeffrey Wildfogel, Ph.D.

It is 15 minutes before your presentation. Your mind is racing. "What if they don't like me? What if they don't participate in my exercises? I can't remember what I'm going to say. I'm so nervous. I know I'm going to bomb."

What causes the greatest pressure for public speakers? To find out, I asked 34 public speakers to name which three of 39 speaking situations, such as, "Microphone not working properly" and "Not having your opening down pat," caused them to feel the most pressure.

The top three pressure-causing situations:

- having peers or colleagues in the audience (32%);

- members of the audience being inattentive (28%);

- not arriving on time (24%).

What can you do to give a powerful presentation when under pressure? In my work as a peak-achievement coach to performers as varied as athletes, belly dancers, salespeople and CEOs, I've discovered similarities in how all peak performers deal with pressure.

- ► They focus on their purpose.
- ► They concentrate only on those things over which they have control.
- ► Keep things in perspective: they know they won't die if they don't do well.
- ► They mentally preview what they want to do, not what they want to avoid doing.
- ► They enjoy themselves.

Here are some tips on how to deal with the key pressure-causing situations.

Speaking before peers—If there are friends in the audience, circulate among them before you speak. During the talk, make eye contact with your friends in order to turn the "scary" audience into a friendly one. If you do not have friends in the audience, make sure to arrive early enough to meet key members of the audience. Getting to know some of them will help you see the audience as a friendly one.

Inattentive audiences—Walk into the audience and talk to those people you met before the presentation. Call them by name and ask them to share stories or thoughts that are relevant to your presentation. This personal touch works well in increasing audience involvement. Another way to get the audience involved is to have them do paired exercises.

Late arrival—Make a quick apology and go on. Use the story of your lateness to illustrate what you are going to talk about. Whatever your topic, there is a story to be told and a lesson to be learned from your arriving late. Find it and use it. You will have demonstrated that you talk about real experiences and that you are a professional under pressure.

A final thought: pressure is an internal state, not an external one. Learn to trust yourself and be present in the moment. Learn to be yourself and don't try to impress the audience. You will then be able to transform pressure into opportunity and deliver your best talk under any circumstance. So go out there, enjoy yourself and knock them alive!

The Business of Speaking

> "How can I trust someone to manage a multi-million dollar project if he or she can't manage a half-hour speech?"
>
> —Bill Hewlett
> Co-founder, Hewlett-Packard Co.

Effective speaking is becoming as important in business today as knowing how to read a balance sheet or prepare a strategic plan. In this age of television, video and teleconferencing, business presenters can no longer retreat into the ". . . Aw shucks . . . unaccustomed as I am to public speaking . . ." excuse for the lack of skills.

This chapter presents ideas for handling a wide range of business speaking situations.

The Business of Speaking

The Seven Myths
of Business Speaking

Bill Johnson (pseudonym) called our office on Wednesday afternoon in a panic. He had a major speech to give Friday morning and wanted help. Bill is vice president of human resources at a fast-growing, Silicon Valley high-tech company.

He was new to the job and had already been called upon to deal with sexual harassment issues in three different cases. His talk Friday was to outline his short- and long-term approach to this highly charged issue. In addition to the entire human resources staff, three vice presidents from other areas and their senior managers were going to be there. Bill was expecting 65 to 70 people in the audience. He was sweating bullets. This was going to be the most critical presentation of his career.

Unfortunately, our respective schedules allowed no time for a meeting. In desperation, he invited me to attend his presentation and prepare a critique. At least we would have a baseline to work from for future improvements.

On Friday morning I attended Bill's 30-minute presentation. His talk lacked energy. His attempts at humor fell flat. People squirmed in their seats. There was a lot of coughing. The audience gave him the standard polite applause. He had bombed, though, and he knew it.

In his desire to persuade his audience, Bill consciously took *himself* out of the speech and became a hollow shell simply reciting facts. There were seven things he did—or rather, failed to do—that dramatically reduced his effectiveness. The mistakes he made were based on hopelessly outmoded ideas he picked up years ago in high school and college public-speaking classes.

These mistakes are so common in business presentations we see today, we've dubbed them "The Seven Myths of Business Speaking."

Myth #1 Avoid the microphone; it's awkward to use. Just project.

Myth #2 Always start with a joke. It warms up the audience.

Myth #3 Never look directly at people—it will make you too nervous. Look above their heads or at the back wall.

Myth #4 Don't use gestures. Arm-waving is distracting.

Myth #5 Stand still when you speak. Moving around makes you look nervous.

Myth #6 Don't get emotional. People are persuaded by logic and facts.

Myth #7 Never, never swear in a speech, it would offend your audience.

Reviewing Bill's talk the next week, we both realized he had been victimized by each of the Seven Myths. He was confused. He followed all of the rules he learned years ago, and yet his talk failed. Bill seemed dejected as he got up to leave the office. I asked why he was so concerned about the problem of sexual harassment.

Playing the devil's advocate, I said, "Aren't most of these accusations coming from women who just want to get even for receiving poor performance reviews?"

He spun on his heel, and in three minutes delivered the most powerful speech I had heard in years. His voice and gestures were strong. He moved around as he spoke and looked me dead in the eye. He was clearly outraged about people being treated this way at work. He also worried about the company's reputation and financial exposure if these allegations were true. He spoke convincingly and he spoke personally.

When he finished, I commented that all he had to do to win the hearts and minds of his next audience was to speak as candidly and as passionately to them. My advice was, "Just be yourself." The trick was, how to do that. Clearly, we had to help him dump those outdated myths about speaking.

In just four weeks, Bill had to address the same audience about what progress was being made. Having this deadline helped with his motivation. He now saw how important it was to get beyond those high school and college myths about speaking.

Myth #1 First Bill practiced using a hand-held microphone. He learned to hold it four to six inches away from his mouth and to grasp it strongly in one hand.

Myth #2 He gave up the opening joke. He decided to begin with a startling statement.

Myth #3 Watching effective speakers and trainers, Bill realized the importance of direct eye interaction with audience members. Looking at the back wall really created more nervousness, not less. He learned the skill of looking directly into the eyes of the audience.

Myth #4 Bill's gestures loosened up naturally as he spoke from his convictions. Small gestures held in close to the body just didn't work. Large gestures did. The strong, one-arm gestures were especially powerful.

Myth #5 Movement away from the lectern had seemed impossible, being both too assertive and off-mic. Now that he could hold the mic he found moving from one side of the room to the other at key transitions in his talk not only possible but effective.

Myth #6 Fired by his personal commitment, the statistics that had been so dry before now took on new meaning. He used stories and delivered them with enthusiasm. He saw that it took more than just facts and logic to persuade an audience.

Myth #7 During one practice session, Bill got so fired up he said, "To hell with this tired excuse that sexual harassment victims bring it on themselves. There is simply no justification for this behavior in our company." Bill paused, stunned by the power of his own rhetoric. He wondered if it was okay to swear. A Bill Cosby quote came to mind: "I don't know the key to success, but the key to failure is trying to please everybody."

Finally the day came for Bill to give his second talk. He approached the lectern confidently. He put down his note cards, pulled the microphone toward him, looked directly at the audience and began: "The cancer of sexual harassment in this company has the potential to put us out of business. It must be stopped now!" You could have heard a pin drop. Every eye was on the speaker.

As he launched into the body of his talk, Bill maintained strong, direct eye contact with audience members as he completed each thought.

People were riveted. I can only describe his gestures as "surgical." He used them to illustrate key ideas and made them big and bold. His stance beside or in front of the lectern made the gestures more powerful. He even added emotional intensity and a couple of swear words. The audience shared his outrage.

In addition to statistics, Bill used stories and anecdotes to get his message across. He talked about the long-term benefits of a work place free of the scourge of sexual harassment. Senior management nodded their approval. The audience was clearly persuaded.

What struck me was how Bill's courage to move beyond the Seven Myths freed him to become himself, and therefore, a persuasive and effective speaker. Good technique and rehearsal had helped a lot. But what sold Bill's audience was not technique, it was his authenticity.

Welcome to the '90s: Speaking to a Culturally Diverse Audience

Contributed by Lu Ellen Schafer

Five minutes before I was scheduled to speak to a group at a high-tech company, the meeting planner said to me, "Oh, by the way, we invited twenty engineers from Asia to listen to your presentation. I'm not sure how much English they know." I hurriedly adjusted my speech to make it more accessible to the visiting engineers. Had I not done so, I would have bombed. As it turned out, they were able to not only get the gist of what I was saying, but also be involved in the audience participation segment. Audiences aren't what they used to be. An increasing percentage of them include foreign-born employees comprised of both foreigners on temporary assignment in the United States and immigrants. With a few minor changes in our presentation, we can fine-tune our delivery so that we are understood by everyone in the audience.

Let's face it. English is not an easy language. It is filled with idioms and slang; to make matters worse, we run our words together. Whaddayathink? sounds

132

nothing like the English taught in Japanese, Korean or Middle Eastern classrooms.

Here are five tips that are guaranteed to make your material more clear and accessible to culturally diverse audiences. While scarcely perceptible to native-born Americans, the changes I am suggesting below will be deeply appreciated by the foreign-born members of the audience. The results you get will far outweigh the effort.

Do Your Homework

Make it a habit to ask in advance if there will be foreign-born participants in the audience. Find out where they are from, and if possible, how long they have been here. Asking these questions will give you helpful information as well as position you as someone aware of current demographics and their impact on the industry.

Slow Down and Use Natural Pauses

Speaking slower . . . with natural pauses . . . will allow everyone . . . a chance to absorb . . . your message . . . Trust me . . . it works like magic.

Saving Face

A Chinese proverb states, "Without face, life is pointless." While no one likes to be humiliated, our culture is much less concerned with saving face than most. We'll often "give it the old college try" and laugh good-naturedly at ourselves. As presenters, however, we must take care to ensure that foreign-born participants never feel the deep shame of losing face while they are in our audience. Here are three pointers:

- ▸ Don't call on foreign-born attendees unless you're sure they understand.

▶ Give the instructions for an activity twice. (This is a good practice with any audience, as it allows you to pick up those who temporarily drifted off.)

▶ During a small group discussion, discreetly circulate to make sure your instructions were understood correctly.

Seeing Is Believing

Use visuals. Be sure that your key points are either on a handout or on the overhead. Spoken English is much harder to follow than written English. If an audience member gets lost, he or she can quickly refer to something in writing.

Watch for Culturally Specific Examples

References to our common culture—the Cosby show, a touchdown, Fourth of July picnics—brighten our presentations and draw the audience in. Many of the references, however, only work for those intimately familiar with our culture. Don't omit them, but sprinkle in stories and references that will resonate with foreign-born participants, too. (Try more "universal" themes such as the joys and challenges of having children, a first trip to a new country, the desire for success, the importance of good friendships.)

Recently, while speaking to a group of American and Taiwanese business people, I used the phrase, "It's a piece of cake." I then turned to the men from Taiwan and said, "Or as you would say, It's like turning over your palm." They were impressed and pleased that I had used a phrase from their own culture, and I'm sure that my credibility rose in their eyes.

All of us strive for the same thing in our speeches and presentations: whether we're addressing an audience of ten in a technical workshop or a crowd of

3,000 at a convention, we want our words to have an impact; we want to make a difference. By adding the above techniques to our repertoire, we markedly increase the chances that all audience members will understand our message and that we will accomplish what we set out to do. As a Peruvian sage wrote: "All is transitory save for the impact we have on each other's lives."

Corporate Employee Meetings with Pizzazz!

Sporting a white wig, marketing director Woody Shackleton sprinted down the aisle at Network Equipment Technology's "All Hands" company meeting. He did his best imitation of Phil Donahue as he interviewed shills in the audience with rehearsed humorous material. The questions and answers related to company issues and drew gales of laughter. An example:

Q: "What does ISO 9000* mean?"

A: "I swear zero defects . . . by the year 9000!"

Why would a company create such a diversion from the "real business" of an all-company meeting? Communication and morale, for starters.

The company's CEO, Dan Warmenhoven, knows how critical these all-employee meetings are to the success of the company. He was determined to maximize the communication value and enjoyment of the meetings. With those goals in mind, Dan began working with our company in early 1991. What we have learned in the production of these employee meetings may be of help to your organization.

*ISO 9000 is an international quality standard being adopted by many American companies.

Executive Pain

Only when senior executives are convinced that the old way of communicating to employees isn't working (i.e., overhead-driven recitations of numerical data) will a change be made. A new approach to communication can't work without top-level support.

Employee Participation

Of course, the content of corporate communication meetings will be determined at the executive level, but the planning and delivery of the program can be handled by both management and non-management staff. This can add variety to meetings that may have become all too predictable.

The "Creative Committee"

In planning humorous segments, remarkable things happen when you get people together who know the company and have a well-developed sense of humor. Be inclusive. Get people from marketing, R & D, administration, sales and manufacturing. Use brainstorming. A lot of the ideas won't work. Those that do, though, will likely be better than one person could generate alone.

Benefits of Participation

When senior-level people give up some of the control of these corporate meetings, they make a strong statement about trust and about participative management. The employees who get involved also get recognition and a sense of inside knowledge about what's going on. Most people are eager to be involved.

Format Variation

People will look forward to meetings that are interesting and a bit unpredictable. At one meeting, Dan invited four people from very different segments of the company to report on how they saw the year progressing. At another meeting, a major customer shared his experience with the company. A third meeting involved a takeoff on the Johnny Carson "Tonight" show. We brought in a band, featuring a "Doc Severinsen" trumpet player. Dan did a Carson-style monologue about the year in review, then interviewed a series of "guests" (employees) who spoke from their perspectives.

Corporate meetings such as these can be critical in getting employee buy-in to ongoing programs. Dan said:

"People used to find All Hands Meetings an imposition. Now they look forward to them. The interest level is much higher now, and so is the level of motivation. People know what the company is doing, and what they need to do to keep N.E.T. growing."

Know the Culture

The key to a successful meeting is input from representative groups around the company. A more entertaining format works best when it reflects real issues people care about; otherwise, it's just a diversion. You will have to determine what works best in your own environment.

Promoting Yourself and Your Business Through Speaking

Contributed by Robert Middleton

If you're a consultant, lawyer, accountant or professional of any kind, you know moving up in your career takes successful "personal marketing." Typically, selling yourself takes the form of membership involvement in organizations, staying in touch with your network and, of course, gaining a reputation for excellent work.

I've noticed, however, that one of the most powerful methods of personal marketing is frequently avoided altogether. I'm talking about public speaking. Fear and a lack of skill are often given as reasons for avoiding this valuable marketing tool, but it usually comes down to the fact that people just don't know where to start.

Beyond Promotion

Promoting yourself through speaking has numerous benefits: positioning yourself as an expert in a particular area, saving time by connecting with many people at once and developing a large pool of prospective clients from your audience. An added benefit is that the process of organizing a presentation relative to your profession adds to the depth of your knowledge and increases your confidence.

There are many opportunities for public speaking. Most of them don't pay anything, but that's not the intent here. Business and service organizations, college extension classes, conferences and alumni groups frequently are looking for speakers.

Getting Booked

To get booked, use a very straightforward approach: call, mail and call again. Call to locate the decision-maker in the organization. Say you have a topic that might be of interest to their group and ask to mail some information. Next mail a package containing the following: a cover letter giving an overview of your topic and why you think the group would be interested, a short professional biography and a short write-up on your topic suitable for reprinting in their newsletter (they'll often reprint it verbatim). Also include any brochures or marketing materials that demonstrate your professionalism.

Finally, call back in a few days, see if they are interested and talk schedules. Some groups plan a month in advance, some six months or more. But the talks most difficult to book frequently are the best. Persistence in follow-up really pays off here.

Making the Talk Count

When you give your talk, make it informative and useful to the audience—not an extended sales pitch. Practice your talk many times, especially before your first presentation. Include audience participation if possible. Leave time for questions and answers. Always promote yourself in an understated way: "If you would like to receive my newsletter, please give me your business card."

You may not be the world's best the first time out, but with practice you'll discover that speaking to promote your business is not only profitable, it can be a whole lot of fun.

Business Speaking:
Boredom or Impact?

Imagine this scene: Your company has sent you to an important three-day technical conference. A nationally recognized authority you have been wanting to hear is introduced.

She has two carousels of 35mm slides. The lights go down. She plants herself behind the lectern and begins reading her speech. The detailed word-slides flip by. You fight to stay awake. The next day you can't remember anything she said.

What a waste. A waste of time and a waste of money. In today's business environment, we simply can no longer afford to have lifeless, boring presentations by speakers who are knowledgeable, though unprepared. There is too much at stake. Ineffective presentations are bad for business, bad for careers, and ultimately, bad for the country. Business meetings are where decisions get made. An essential part of American competitiveness is our ability to communicate internally and with our customers. Our ability to speak effectively, get things done and sell our products and ideas is central to the vitality of our economy. Being able to present our ideas persuasively in front of others is as important as the ideas themselves.

Yet, many business and technical speakers feel uncomfortable being "on stage." They are not, after all, trained entertainers. So they may hide behind the detailed content and do not take time to rehearse. The result? A technically accurate presentation that falls flat.

What can people do to have greater impact in business and technical speaking?

► Take presentations seriously. Make time for them.

► Get training. It is a learned skill.

► Practice, practice, practice.

Acting vs. Speaking

Occasionally in a PowerSpeaking® program, someone will say: "This is just acting technique." Is it just acting? What are the differences or similarities between acting and speaking?

First of all, both actors and speakers are performing. Both want to keep their audience's attention. The similarity ends there. An actor portrays a character he is not. An actor uses someone else's (the playwright's) words. Speakers are themselves, and they speak their own words. When you speak, it's your point of view you express. It's very demanding to be yourself, not just a character.

The goals of speakers and actors are quite different. A speaker wants to connect personally with the audience. Actors perform in front of an audience; interaction is not the goal. Take eye interaction, for example. A speaker needs direct, sustained eye contact to both build credibility and get feedback. Typically, an actor focuses on other actors, not the audience.

The main difference, though, is intent. When you, as a business presenter, speak before customers, senior management, or your staff meeting, big things can happen: sales, product launches, hiring decisions or capital equipment purchases. The economy and people's lives are affected. Something important happens. Actors, on the other hand, are entertainers, and only occasionally perform in a work that has an effect on people's lives.

As you admire and learn from the talent of show business greats, keep in mind that when they perform, we are entertained. When you perform, the economy moves and the wheels of progress turn. Here's your Oscar.

PowerSpeaking® Helps Land Big Sale

On December 13, 1991 Linda Wallace made, perhaps, the most important presentation of her life. On December 17, her company, Rucker Fuller, an office furniture supply company, was awarded a $3,000,000 contract to be spread over three years. The client commented later that the presentation had been a critical part of their decision to buy from Rucker Fuller. What was behind this winning presentation?

Because Rucker Fuller's management knew that excellent presentation skills are critical in today's cost-conscious, highly competitive sales environment, they made an investment in training. They decided not only to train sales reps in PowerSpeaking®, but also to work extensively with our associate, Melinda Henning. Melinda helped them define their sales strategy, sales language and storytelling to highlight the company's history and quality. In April, Linda Wallace took the two-day PowerSpeaking® training. In November, she attended Melinda's half-day session on storytelling.

Linda's presentation was to a San Francisco-based law firm. With over 450 employees in four California locations, the client was upgrading its offices and needed lots of new furniture. They opened the bidding to three companies. Each group had just 30 minutes to make their pitch. In a word, pressure!

Linda began by meeting with her management to go over the core message, "You can depend on Rucker Fuller" and several key points that were supported by Rucker Fuller stories. She crafted the presentation, then gave it to the sales staff and received valuable feedback. She had one more dry run with senior management. While other Rucker Fuller people also presented at the meeting, Linda did most of it. She included visuals, which helped the client see what Rucker Fuller could do for them.

During those critical 30 minutes in front of the client, Linda's preparation really paid off. It's not enough to have high-quality products and services. Wins like this also take outstanding presentation skills and lots of preparation. The Rucker Fuller management is also to be congratulated for putting its resources into staff training. They got an excellent return on investment and the payoff will be long-term.

The Technology of Speaking

> *"Don't tell me the details of how you got the data, just tell me what the data means."*
> —Ralph Patterson
> Hewlett-Packard
>
> *"My purpose is to make sure people hear the message and don't get lost in the details."*
> —Ken Braly
> Computer Consultant
>
> *"We can get information all day and night. What we need is knowledge."*
> —Steve Schramm
> General Magic

The engine of our economy is manufacturing. The fuel for that engine is technology. New products are dreamed up and developed, usually, by scientists and engineers in R & D labs sprinkled throughout the Fortune 500 and all the way down to small start-up companies. A good technical presentation can be a first step in the development of a new product.

This chapter is about the technical presentation and some of the more technical aspects of speaking.

The Technical Presentation

"The mark of a truly educated person is to be moved deeply by statistics."
—George Bernard Shaw

Myths About Technical Talks

- Content is everything. Style is unimportant.
- Technical people are very bright, so it's okay to do a data dump.
- The overhead projector is more important than the speaker.
- Enthusiasm is offensive. Analytical people expect boring presentations.
- Technical talks are simply informational; they're not meant to be persuasive.

The tone of the technical presentation is impersonal, objective. The content is often data, statistics and facts. The tricky part is that this objective information has to be presented to subjective human beings. To hold their attention and get their buy-in, the technical presenter must draw on general principles of human communication. The first is to make the content easy to understand.

151

Signal-to-Noise Ratio

Imagine you are driving on a remote country road and turn on your car radio. You hear a faint signal and lots of intermittent static. Very frustrating. Contrast this to listening to your compact disc player at home. No static, just clean sound.

Interference in an electrical transmission is called "noise." Too much noise and the signal or message won't be received. Likewise, in speaking, our objective is to have the audience receive our signal loud and clear, with minimal noise in the system. What is "noise" in a presentation? An unclear message; hard-to-read visual aids; nervous mannerisms, etc.

Since technical talks are so information-dense, the main message can get buried in an avalanche of detail. The listeners get overwhelmed and simply tune out. Little is remembered.

The accompanying chart is an effective way to evaluate the success of a technical talk. The presenter's goal is to increase the signal and decrease the noise.

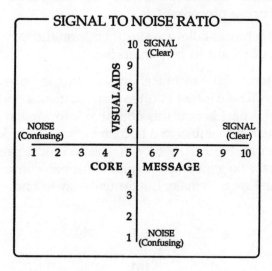

If the core message is easy to identify and does not get confused with background information, give a high score. If the visual aids are clear, easy to understand and help support the core message, give a high score. The goal, of course, is to get a 10/10.

HP Laboratories Survey

Recently, we conducted a survey at Hewlett-Packard Laboratories in Palo Alto, California to determine what technical presenters wanted to hear from other presenters. We found that rather than wanting more technical detail, they wanted more concise organization, more effective style and better visual aids (usually overhead transparencies).

Contrary to conventional wisdom that says the technical audience is eager for a "data dump," our survey results reflect people's concern that talks be well organized and easy to follow. Technical speakers who try to show how much they know by making their presentation complex would be more successful if they focused instead on simplifying the message. It's a classic example of "less is more." Simplifying and repeating the "core message" will result in increased buy-in and retention.

In addition, we know that audiences pay more attention during openings and conclusions. These crucial segments are often ignored by technical presenters who prefer to jump right into the body of the presentation and start immediately discussing the data. They need to give the audience a reason to listen in the opening and have a strong memorable close. The speaker's core message will get across in these segments.

Business or technical audiences have a lot on their minds. They are not paying full attention to the presentation. To be remembered, the message must be simple and it must be repeated. If there is too much extraneous background data or if the flow of thought is unclear, this "noise" in the system will cause people to tune out.

Delivery Style

Technical audiences are especially skeptical of too much style and enthusiasm. They expect focus on the content, not a "rah-rah" motivational talk. On the other hand, it's also true that they find boring presentations to be frustrating and a waste of time.

Often the technical presenter is very uncomfortable in the speaking situation and so prefers to hide behind the data. Unfortunately, a shy, academic, tentative delivery style will ruin the speaker's effectiveness. Like any other speaker, a technical presenter will be far more persuasive when he or she masters the simple elements of powerful style: stance, movement, gesture, voice, pause and eye interaction.

Visual Aids

Technical presenters historically have relied too much on overhead transparencies and people often find them distracting and boring. It's an all too familiar scene: a technical expert stands next to the overhead projector with a huge pile of transparencies, reading each hard-to-read visual to a half-sleeping audience. This is referred to as the talking overhead projector.

So what's the solution? Eliminate visual aids? Not at all. Technical talks by nature are overhead-driven: flow charts, complex diagrams, equations. Here are some ways to hold your audience's attention, even with complex visuals:

- ► use fewer rather than more;
- ► use color graphs and charts rather than word slides;

- ► don't begin or end the talk with visuals;
- ► keep visuals big and bold.

Summary

Technical presentations are similar to, and different from, non-technical presentations. They are different in that they focus on physical events or data rather than people. The technical audience already has specialized knowledge about the topic. Like any audience, though, their time is valuable and they don't want to be bored.

To make your next technical presentation successful, remember these guidelines:

- ► deliver the talk with enough style and audience involvement to keep them interested;
- ► keep the content clear and the organization easy to follow;
- ► reduce the number of visual aids and keep them big, bold and colorful.

Finally, remember signal-to-noise ratio. Nobody likes to hear a radio program with static.

Computer-Generated Graphics: Use with Caution

A recent study conducted by the 3M Visual Systems Division indicates that some of the hot, exciting presentation graphics programs may be overkill. When not used with care, the newer presentation formats can actually detract from audience retention.

When on-screen, real-time effects are used, keep them simple, the study indicates. These findings were summarized in the September, 1992 issue of *Meeting Management News*:

▸ According to the new research, audiences respond best to a speaker who uses technology as a presentation aid. Response declines rapidly when the speaker takes a back seat to complex on-screen visuals that appear "canned" to the audience.

▸ Key points in the research report show that presenters can improve the audience's perception of their presentation with:

Simple computer-generated graphics. Whether displayed on an overhead projector, projection panel or monitor, these graphics boosted the audience's perception of the speaker as well as its comprehension and retention—so long as the chart conveyed relevant data. Not surprisingly, "art" added to presentations with little linkage to the topic being presented detracted from the audience's understanding of the presentation.

Animation. A glitzy multimedia presentation won't help an unprepared speaker impress his or her audience, the research project found. But a good speaker can use animation very effectively to boost audience retention. The most effective animations proved to be among the simplest, such as bar charts that grow or text revealed line by line.

So, when you are tempted to use your portable computer and liquid crystal display panel on top of the overhead projector to really wow 'em, remember to keep it simple. You are still the star of the show. Your visual aids are just that—aids.

Let's Not Get Lost in the Technology

Contributed by Steven Kirsch

As vice president of a company that makes desktop publishing software, I recently delivered an unusual message to a large audience of people who use computer-aided publishing tools.

The message was simply this: we need to remember not to get carried away by the technology. Better looking overhead transparencies and 35mm slides don't necessarily mean more effective communication.

With the variety of desktop publishing and presentation tools available today, it's easy to believe that our presentations will be better just because we use these tools. Nothing could be further from the truth.

These tools can help you produce legible slides and reasonable-looking documents quickly and easily. No more, no less. But that's really all you need.

We have to remember that the point is not how to make better slides, the point is how to give better presentations. So after you've purchased your software, if you really want to communicate better, get some training on how to give more effective presentations!

People spend hours and hours preparing their visuals. But most of us haven't spent any time at all learning how to use the simple, effective presentation tools we were born with. Just a few hours of professional coaching on the effective use of gestures, eye contact, voice, staging, organization and content can make a world of difference.

I mean, what good are good-looking slides if half your audience is asleep?

Visual Aids Do Not a Presentation Make

The hum of the overhead projector. The glare on the screen. The monotone voice. Your eyes are getting heavy. You fight to stay awake.

Overhead transparencies (or slides) are the most used and abused visuals in business today. They are appealing because they are inexpensive to prepare and easy to use. Recent studies by the 3M Company showed that presenters are 43% more credible when they use visuals. Visuals should highlight or outline your talk. They are an effective way to present information that can't be described verbally, e.g., a schematic or flow chart.

Nervous speakers will often use visuals as a way to shift attention away from themselves. This is a mistake, since it is ultimately the speaker that persuades the audience, not the visuals.

Follow these simple guidelines to have success with overhead transparencies:

Design:	***Keep it Big and Bold***
	Horizontal format
	One idea per slide
	No more than six lines per slide
	No more than six words per line

Letters 3/8"-1/2" in height (never typed)

Use colors

Use diagrams, cartoons or other graphics

Hold slides in "flip frames" (3M)

Preparation: ***Attend To Details***

Arrive early to get familiar with equipment

Adjust projector; distance to screen; focus image

Place first transparency on projector

Sequence transparencies for the presentation

Delivery: ***Take Charge***

Rehearse the delivery, incorporating visuals

Talk to audience before showing transparencies

Walk around projector

Stand flush with the screen

Point to screen, not transparency

Turn off projector when not in use

Do not cover part of the slide to control audience's attention

Talk to audience, not to screen

Turn off projector before conclusion

Overhead Research

Effects of Overhead Use in Business Meetings:

(Wharton Study, The Wharton Applied Research Center, University of Pennsylvania, 1981)

- ► Shorter meetings (reduced length by 28%)
- ► Faster group decisions

- ▸ Perception of a more professional, credible presenter
- ▸ Increase in understanding by participants (50% better retention rate)
- ▸ More decisions made at meetings

Effects of Visuals During Presentations:
(University of Minnesota/3M Study, 1985)

- ▸ Presentations with visuals 43% more persuasive
- ▸ Color more persuasive than black and white
- ▸ 35mm slides heighten sense of professionalism
- ▸ Overhead transparencies heighten interest in the presenter
- ▸ Visuals add clarity, interest

VISUAL AIDS		
TYPE	**PRO**	**CON**
Flip Chart	Easy to use Informal Audience participa- tion Low Tech Spontaneous	Small groups only Back to audience Illegible printing Spelling problems
Overhead Projector	Inexpensive Room lights on Versatile Control of equipment Presenter faces audience Easy to edit Personal involvement Color	Overuse Noisy Overly common

35 mm
Slide
Projector
	Professional look,
	  impact
	Variety
	Photographic clarity
	Use with larger
	  audiences
	Colorful and exciting
		Dim room lights
		Technical difficulties
		Difficult to take notes
		More impersonal
		Difficult to edit

Handouts	Provide detail	Distraction
Props	High interest Touch Graphic interest Audience involve- ment	Distraction

Graphically Speaking

Contributed by Mary McGlynn

Using a visual aid? Remember this: your audience will get your information quicker if you present it in a graphic rather than tabular or written form. Here are five common ways to show information in a graph. (For more information see: *Say It With Charts* by Gene Zelazny, Dow Jones-Irwin, Homewood, IL, 1985.)

TYPE	GOAL	GUIDELINE
PIE CHART	Size of each part as a percentage of a total	No more than six components
BAR CHART	Comparison of how items rank	Make spaces smaller than bar width
COLUMN CHART	Change over time or Frequency change	Use column chart with fewer items
LINE CHART	Change over time or Frequency change	Use to show trend Trend line darker than baseline
SCATTERGRAM	Relationship between variables	Use to show pattern of correlation

"They Didn't Want Statistics . . ."

Contributed by Steve Schramm

My most difficult situation occurred early in my career. I was to give a technical talk to a large group of senior, experienced engineers. I did a lot of research, collected statistics and organized a speech that I thought was very detailed. I thought it would be impressive to the audience. After about ten minutes of rattling off information it was obvious that the audience was disinterested and bored. I was blowing it big time. I went another minute or two jumping to what I thought were interesting points, but no change.

I handled it by stopping my speech, looking out into the audience and saying, "I can see that what I'm saying is not what you wanted or expected—what were you hoping for?"

After a pause, when people realized I wasn't going to continue, one person said that they didn't want statistics—they wanted real examples from situations I had seen or experienced. When other people agreed, I related some experiences and invited the audience to also share some personal stories, which they did. It went much better for the rest of the hour.

"Oh Yeah? . . . Says Who?" Things We Know *For Sure* About Speaking

"Content is only worth 7% of your total impact as a speaker."

Oh yeah? Says who? Aphorisms like this are often presented to trainees as gospel out on the "slippery slopes" of human communications training. Don't believe everything you hear.

The source of the above statement is the work of Dr. Albert Mehrabian, a social psychologist at UCLA. The statement is often misrepresented. It's used in presentations training to convince participants of the importance of nonverbal communication. The problem is, it is largely irrelevant. Mehrabian's work focused on interpersonal communications—not public speaking.

Like everyone else in the presentations training field, we have a certain point of view about what speakers should do to maximize their effectiveness. Much of this is based on personal experience, hunches and observations. Some of it, though, is based on actual empirical studies. What follows are things we know for sure about speaking because they have been documented in the scientific literature.

Substance

Fact: People remember longer and learn more quickly material at the beginning and at the end of a presentation.

Application: State your core message loud and clear at the beginning and at the end of your talk.

Source: Crowder, R., "Auditory and Temporal Factors in the Modality Effect," *Journal of Experimental Psychology*, Vol. 12, No. 2, 1986, pp. 268-278.

Fact: Speech retention is enhanced by core message repetition.

Application: Repeat your core message at least three times during your talk.

Source: Ross, Raymond S., *Understanding Persuasion*, Prentice Hall, Englewood Cliffs, NJ, 1990, p. 162.

Fact: Stories have stronger impact than statistics.

Application: Include stories, applications or examples to illustrate your statistical information.

Source: Martin, J. and Powers, M., "Organizational Stories: More Vivid and Persuasive than Quantitative Data," in *Psychological Foundations of Organizational Behavior*, Barry Staw, Ed., 1983.

Style

Fact: Delivery (style) has more impact than content, organization or visual aids.

Application: Develop a confident delivery style. Take time to rehearse.

Source: Weaver, R. (Air Force Institute of Technology, Wright-Patterson AFB, OH), "Delivery: Forty Percent of Technical Briefing Effectiveness," Paper, Society for Technical Communication, Denver, CO, May, 1987.

❖ ❖ ❖

Fact: Of all the speaker's style techniques, eye contact is the most powerful influencer of comprehension and credibility.

Application: Learn to look directly into the eyes of audience members for extended periods —like the completion of an entire thought, or core message.

Source: Beebe, S., "Effects of Eye Contact Posture, and Vocal Inflection Upon Credibility and Comprehension," Paper delivered to the Speech Communication Association Convention, 1978.

Fact: People who are lying use few gestures (if any), fidget, speak fast and have a high vocal pitch.

Application: To increase credibility, speak in a lower tone, speak slower and use expansive "Zone II" gestures.

Source: Ekman, P., *Telling Lies*, Berkeley Books, New York, 1985.

❖ ❖ ❖

Fact: Deep, regular breathing reduces anxiety.

Application: Decrease speech nervousness by breathing deeply before you go on.

Source: Longo, D. and vom Saal, W., "Respiratory Relief Therapy: A New Treatment for the Reduction of Anxiety," *Behavior Modification*, July, 1984, pp. 361- 378.

❖ ❖ ❖

Fact: What, when, and how much you eat dramatically affects your speech performance.

Application: Eat a light meal of protein and carbohydrates no more than two hours before your speech. Do not eat fats.

Source: Wurtman, J., "Preperformance Meals: Eating for a Winning Presentation," in *Managing Your Mind and Mood Through Food*, pp. 121-143, Rawson Associates, New York, 1986.

❖ ❖ ❖

Fact: Mental practice can increase your actual performance.

Application: Visualize yourself delivering an outstanding presentation as you prepare. Intersperse visualization with rehearsal.

Source: Swets, J. and Bjork, R., "Enhancing Human Performance: An Evaluation of 'New Age' Techniques Considered by the U. S. Army," *Psychological Science*, March, 1990, pp. 85-96.

Staging

Fact: Using visual aids increases the audience's retention of your presentation by 55%.

Application: Enhance your spoken message with visual aids. (Warning: do not over-use visuals or audience attention may fade quickly.)

Source: Zayas-Baya, E., "Instructional Media in the Total Language Picture," *International Journal of Instructional Media 5*, 1977-1978, pp. 145-150.

Technical Wiz at 30 . . . Speaking Pro at 50

Fact: Because of the nature of brain physiology, we are better at working out abstract, complex problems in our youth, but slowly lose that skill with age. Applied skills that demand interpretation, wisdom and judgment improve with age. The ability to speak and write improves from age 50 to 70.

Application: Cheer up: there are some benefits to aging.

Source: Mark, V. and Mark, J., *Brain Power*, Houghton Mifflin, Boston, MA, 1989.

So, remember, the next time some communications guru makes a wild statement about eye contact, visual aids, or content you just say . . . "Oh yeah? Says who?"

The Impact of Music

A jumpy rhythm makes you feel so fine.
It'll shake all your troubles
from your worried mind.

—Johnny Cash

Ever considered using music for your training sessions or speaking dates? It adds grace and harmony to any program. It relaxes participants and helps to break the ice. With today's technology, it is inexpensive to provide high-quality music.

The Source—Use a small, portable cassette tape player ($50 - $100) and two compact detachable speakers ($100/pair). Everything is battery powered.

The Music*—Use judgment here—nothing too far-out. The sound should be upbeat and acceptable to a general audience. What's worked well for us: classical (e.g., Bach's Brandenburg Concertos, Vivaldi, etc.) and "new age" (Paul Horn, Windham Hill, Leo Kottke, etc.).

Experiment—People will let you know soon enough what music works and what doesn't. Oh, one more thing—the music will help save your sanity, too.

*Note: If you play music in a public forum (like a speech or training workshop) you are required to pay a use fee to ASCAP or BMI. Contact these agencies directly for more information.

Microphones: What You Don't Know *Can* Hurt You

Contributed by Mary McGlynn

Tap . . . Tap . . . Tap. "Can you hear me in the back?"

"I don't need a mic. My voice will carry."

Head down to microphone level, leaning forward, "Ah . . . ah . . . is this on?"

Microphones have the potential to turn a speech into a nightmare for the speaker and the audience. Good microphone technique separates the amateur from the pro. The effective use of a mic will add to your presentation success.

Major Types of Microphones

Hand-Held—A hand-held mic is the workhorse of all microphones. It is designed to be touched and can take some rough treatment. It should be held six to twelve inches from your mouth at a 45-degree angle or less. If held vertically, it may pick up feedback from the ceiling loudspeakers. If held too close to the mouth, the speaker may produce annoying hissing and popping.

An important speaking skill is comfort using the hand-held microphone. Usually this type of mic is held in a goose-neck holder attached to the lectern. Prior to the talk take control by:

► pulling the microphone out of the goose-neck to develop a sense of ease, control and smoothness;

► checking the length of cord available when you move away from the lectern;

► practicing a portion of your talk with the volume controls set so that you sense the relationship between your varying vocal levels and the position of your mic. Remember, as you move your head, move the mic.

With a hand-held microphone it is critical to be aware of the placement of the loudspeakers in the room. To avoid feedback, stay *behind* the speakers.

Clip-on—There is good news and bad news. The good news is that clip-on mics give you freedom to gesture, to operate equipment, to point to items—to get involved in the talk. The bad news is that they are prone to feedback, have a less stable sound quality and are more fragile.

The lapel mic clips onto your tie, shirt or blouse about four inches below your mouth. It has a cord that leads to a connector (usually attached to the speaker's belt), which in turn has a cord leading to the public address system. When walking with the microphone, watch the cord. Grab it, control it and don't let it intimidate you. The loose cord leading to the connector at your belt can be hidden under a blouse or shirt or just put in your pants or skirt pocket.

For women: wear a jacket and a blouse with buttons so you have a place to attach the mic. Avoid jewelry that interferes with the mic. Both men and women should minimize noise coming from clothing rubbing against the mic.

Wireless—Nothing to restrict freedom of movement; no cords to trip over. Sounds like heaven, doesn't it? These mics can be hand-held or lavaliere types. The disadvantage of the wireless mic is the vulnerability to competing radio signals. Also, they can cause you embarrassment if you forget to turn them off after leaving the stage.

Microphone Use

After considering which mic to use, the next issue is how to use it effectively. Here are some tips that will give you the look of a pro:

- ► Use your normal tone of voice; there's no need to yell.

- ► Test the system in advance. Go to the room early and test on your own time, not the audience's time. Try on the mic. Move with it. Make it your own. Check the volume levels. Know where the loudspeakers are so that you can avoid feedback.

- ► Do not blow into a microphone. Test it by snapping your fingers, counting—but not blowing.

- ► Before saying the first word, adjust the microphone to your satisfaction.

- ► Keep the hand-held mic near your mouth, even when you turn your head, otherwise, you'll go "off mic."

- ► Avoid holding the mic with both hands and change hands with the mic occasionally.

- ► Use a mic when there are 50 or more people in your audience.

Finally, it boils down to this: if the audience can hear your message better with a mic, use one.

How to Record
Your Presentations

You put weeks into the preparation of your talk. The audience loved it. You got your message across and you feel great. Now what?

If you did not record your talk, all you have left are memories. If, however, you taped your speech, you have a way to build on the work you put into it. There are at least three reasons why you should record your presentations:

- ▶ to review it to improve your substance and style;
- ▶ to edit the tape and use it to show others what you can do (i.e., make a "demo tape");
- ▶ to draw on the content for future talks.

The question is, how do you get a good recording without hiring a sound technician? There is a simple answer: wear your recording equipment on your body.

Recording technology has advanced to the point where it is now very easy and relatively inexpensive for you to get studio-quality live recordings of all your presentations. Here are some tips on how to record your talks.

Tape Recorder—Use a small "auto reverse" tape recorder. After reaching the end of the tape, auto reverse allows the machine to continue recording. This way you can record 45 minutes in each direction on a 90-minute cassette without needing to stop and turn the cassette over. (Never use tapes longer than C90s. Longer tapes are thinner and may get eaten by the cassette recorder.) Always use full-size cassette tapes, not the micros. The smaller cassettes are more difficult to edit and the size is not universal.

Microphone—Use a condenser microphone with built-in-battery for maximum fidelity and sensitivity. These mics have a battery to boost their sensitivity. Place the mic about six inches below your mouth on your tie or lapel. It picks up audience response as well as your voice.

Wearing Your Recorder—The advantage of the small auto-reverse tape recorders is that they can be worn on your belt or in a pocket with ease.

Wearing your recording equipment has several advantages. You have complete freedom of movement, and you don't have to depend on someone else to do your taping.

Another way to get a quality recording is to tape directly from the PA system. Of course this eliminates the necessity for you to wear a tape recorder. If you use an auto-reverse recorder, you will not need help. If, however, you use a standard professional recorder, a recording engineer or a colleague will need to turn the tape over after 45 minutes.

Pitfalls—There is a speaker's "law of the universe" that guarantees it will be your very best presentation when the batteries go dead or you plug the mic into the "headphones" jack. Pay special attention to small details.

I recently decided not to record a major presentation to 200 colleagues because it was being "recorded professionally." The technician stopped recording after my summary, thereby eliminating my final story, the musical ending and the applause. So remember to get good quality tapes to show to others, and to use for self-critique, record everything you do with equipment you wear on your person. This will ensure that all the work and preparation result in more than just memories after the standing ovation is over.

The Biology of Speaking

> *"Right now, at this very moment, for better or for worse, the food you ate at your last meal or snack is affecting your mood and behavior."*
> —*Judith Wurtman, Ph.D.*
> *Nutritionist*

The vehicle for getting your message across is your body. Managing your diet and caring for your voice can pay off in successful presentations. This chapter tells you how.

A Speaker's Diet

At 9:30 AM John gave his presentation to senior management. The future of his project and his department hung in the balance. He started slowly and went downhill from there. He felt heavy, unable to collect his thoughts. While everyone was polite enough, he did not get the funding he requested.

What happened? Was he unprepared? Was he too nervous? Were his biorhythms off that day? Any of these things could be true. What is more likely, though, is that the rich, cream-filled Danish he ate at 8:15 AM did him in.

Judith J. Wurtman, Ph.D., in her 1986 book, *Managing Your Mind and Mood Through Food*, has an entire chapter on eating strategies for making winning presentations. Her suggestions include:

Eat Light—Avoid heavy, rich meals before you present; however, don't starve yourself. You need food in your system for energy.

Time Your Meals—Plan to eat about two hours before you speak so most digestion will be complete when you take center stage.

Eat Low-Fat, Low Calorie Foods—High calorie, high-fat foods are harder to digest and divert blood to the digestive process. Include carbohydrates and protein for greater mental alertness during your presentation.

Wurtman's book offers other tips, including conference and banquet eating, avoiding jet lag through diet and eating to ease stress.

Blood Sugar
and Your Performance

Contributed by Maureen Sullivan

Ever stood up to speak and found your mouth dry, your mind blank and your heart pounding? Chances are, most of us have experienced some of these symptoms. They are physiological manifestations of stress.

For many people, speaking in public is stressful. Even those of us who enjoy speaking may experience symptoms associated with stress before, during or after a talk.

This stress reaction may wreak havoc on your blood sugar, causing both physical and emotional reactions.

For a controlled, confident performance, use the following tips to prevent low blood sugar. First of all, avoid sugar, alcohol and overly refined foods. They break down too quickly, causing an insulin response which then exacerbates your existing stress. Concentrate on protein foods for the morning (eggs, meat, poultry), combined with complex carbohydrates (whole grains, bread, fruits, rice, potatoes, vegetables). Fresh fruit (for example, an apple a half hour prior to speaking) will give you a lift that should carry you through your talk.

Do not increase your caffeine consumption the day of your talk.

Keep your dietary habits consistent because radical changes will cause an imbalance. After your talk, another piece of fruit will help stabilize your blood sugar. Try sprinkling protein powder on the fruit for an even longer-lasting effect.

If you integrate this into your preparation for public speaking, you will have control over your blood sugar, rather than it controlling you.

Care and Feeding of Your Voice

Contributed by Jerry Johnson

Commercial radio broadcasting has been my career for twenty-five years. I have been on-air talent, newsman, TV and radio talk-show host and an executive with ABC radio.

Over the years, I've discovered many things about the voice. People frequently abuse it. The following cautions will help you take better care of your voice.

Voice Hazards

Dairy Products—Milk products contribute to the build-up of phlegm and mucus (frogs in your throat) particularly if consumed before a speech. If you're nervous, the problem is worse.

Vocal Strain—The vocal apparatus is very delicate. Any type of strain, whether yelling at a football game or compensating for a bad PA system, results in hoarseness, laryngitis or worse.

Strong Throat Sprays—A newscaster colleague once lost his voice for a month after "pushing it" through a sore throat by using a strong spray. Vocal cords are delicate tissues that need TLC, not punishment from chemical band-aids.

Smoke—If you speak a lot and still smoke . . . what's there to say? Smoker's throat, smoker's cough and the sound of a voice that has been tortured with smoke should convince anyone that smoke is cruel and unusual punishment for the voice.

Coffee and Hot Tea—Both contribute to the dryness of throat and mouth tissue, which is especially bad just before making a presentation or speech.

Voice Treatments

Hot Water—Drink it all the time. I have used it in place of coffee for years and it's great! Hot water has a taste and is terrific for your vocal apparatus (and entire body). You can also add some lemon. At a speech or presentation, I request plenty of hot water. It works!

Salt Water—This is absolutely the best treatment for a sore throat. Do it frequently, every half-hour if possible. It is also a good treatment just before giving a speech, a meeting or a major sales presentation.

Steam—Breathe hot steam into your mouth, nose and lungs. This is the best treatment I've ever found for hoarseness, sore vocal cords and laryngitis. Hot steam from a shower will do, but I get better results from a tea kettle on the stove. Drape a towel over your head, inhale the steam for as long as you can, take a break, then do it again. You'll feel the results almost immediately. The secret is moisture and heat. Your voice loves both.

Throat Lozenges—Use good quality, gentle, but effective throat lozenges. Many of the popular products are not worth buying, in my opinion. The best one I know of is Ricola Swiss Herb Candy, imported by Richter Bros., Inc. Look for it in drug stores, health food stores and supermarkets.

An ABC colleague of mine was assigned to cover Britain's military action in the Falkland Islands. He was away more than three weeks and punished his voice daily. He got chilled on shore and aboard ship. He didn't get much sleep, smoked steadily, never stopped talking and frequently shouted to make himself heard over poor telephone lines back to the States.

My friend returned very ill. He had an acute case of strep throat with other complications and could not say a single word for six weeks. His voice never fully recovered from the ordeal.

As with so much of life, common sense is crucial. This is especially true on health matters and those related to the voice. As a manager, salesperson or speaker, your voice is your most important asset. We only get one voice. Take good care of yours.

The Future of Speaking

> "The day after I took a PowerSpeaking® workshop, I went on to teach my 30 first-grade students to be speakers. Surprisingly, they enjoyed it and each week they couldn't wait to get up to talk. When these kids reach adulthood, they won't be afraid to speak out."
>
> —Pauline Binkley
> First Grade Teacher

In our PowerSpeaking® training programs we hear countless tales of childhood humiliation in some distant public-speaking nightmare. Often the emotional scars of the experience remain long into adulthood. This does not have to happen. In this chapter we'll meet some adults who believe kids can master this skill and some kids who have.

PowerSpeaking® for Kids

Contributed by John Warren

"Before this class, I was really shy and hardly ever spoke to anyone. Now I can speak freely to people."

"I got a lot out of it and would recommend it to others to overcome nervousness. I learned to stand, gesture and not to appear nervous."

"I was afraid of being laughed at. I'm glad I took the class because it taught me how to be confident and not nervous in front of a group of people, whether they're your friends or not."

This feedback from young speakers reflects the impact of speech training for kids. One of the best ways for you to reinforce the skills you have is to teach them to others. And who better to teach them to than an eager group of kids? You could start at home with your own children and their friends or offer to teach a class at a local school, youth club, recreation center or through a Toastmasters Club.

You can pass the baton of knowledge and skill to the next generation and give them a head start! Start by coaching them on a project or presentation they have to give in class.

191

The gains in both self-confidence and speaking skills coincide with three easy-to-teach behaviors which the students pick up very quickly (quicker than most adults!). First, work on a solid, well-balanced stance. Since most students are taking physical education or are involved in sports, encourage them to use the same balanced stance they would use playing softball, tennis or shooting free-throws in basketball. They understand the analogy of balance right away. Second, encourage them to use gestures to describe the action in their talk. Kids are much less inhibited than adults in this area, especially when they are given permission. Help them learn ways to visualize the words they are saying and help their listeners to "get the picture." Lastly, have them work on making eye interaction with one person at a time in their audience. That tip alone seems to help them get over the fear of speaking to a group.

Your involvement could be as informal as coaching your own kids at home or as structured as a formal class. If the idea of the Toastmasters Youth Leadership Program is of interest to you, you can get more information from your local Toastmasters Club.

The skill and confidence to speak powerfully is not only important to you, it's important to our youth and our future. Share your knowledge, reinforce your skills and pass the baton to others.

How to Get More Practice

Contributed by John Warren

If you have completed the PowerSpeaking® training, you have taken the single-best step to improving your confidence and competence in public speaking. However, presentation skills, like other skills, require ongoing practice if they are to be maintained and developed. With a little effort and advance planning you can turn every speaking opportunity into a practice session from which you can learn and grow.

The best way to get the feedback you need is to have someone videotape your presentation. Later you can review the tape to examine the overall impact.

The next best option is to audio-tape the speech. Audio-tape is readily available and easy to set up. For the best quality recording, attach a lavaliere microphone from the recorder to your clothing, four to six inches from your mouth. When you review the tape, listen especially for the tone and quality of your voice, how effectively you pause and the words you use to illustrate key points.

In addition to the kind of feedback you can get from video and audio-taping your own talks, you can get many more opportunities to speak and sharpen your skills by joining a Toastmasters Club. Dedicated to helping its members improve their speaking, listening and leadership skills, there are literally thousands of Toastmasters clubs around the world and guests are always welcome. Club members are very supportive and can provide you with the opportunity to experiment with your speaking style in a non-threatening environment. For a listing of the Toastmasters clubs near you, contact Toastmasters International, P.O. Box 9052, Mission Viejo, CA 92690-7052 (714) 858-8255.

The time you invest in continued practice and development of your speaking skills will pay big rewards in both increased self-confidence and your ability to influence others by your powerful presentations.

Diana Bock
Knocks Their Socks Off!

Eleven-year-old Diana Bock got up to address 400 professional speakers at the National Speakers Association annual meeting in Palm Desert, California in 1991. She had never spoken in public before. Her voice was shaky. A couple of times she forgot what she was saying. She pushed on.

When she finished, those 400 professional speakers leaped to their feet and gave her a thunderous ovation. Diana's self-confidence soared. Today, she still feels stronger because of that momentary success. What happened?

The trip to the NSA Conference and Diana's participation in the youth program had been planned for some time. Her father, Wally Bock, had encouraged her participation and asked her to think about making a presentation. What to talk about? Diana's best friend, Connie Khamvanthong is from Laos. The story of how Connie and her family got from war-torn Laos to Richmond, California would make a good speech, Diana thought. She was right.

The family's escape was a harrowing experience. The high point was their crossing of a raging river at night to find freedom in neighboring Thailand—the first step to getting to America. One of the boats overturned in the river and many possessions were lost. They almost lost one of their children.

Diana used the river as a metaphor for all the challenges we face in life—all the fearful things we must do—all our inner self-doubts. She had that audience spellbound as she told this gripping story. Obviously nervous throughout her talk, as she ended her brief presentation, she concluded: ". . . and by speaking before you here today, I'm crossing my own river." The audience went nuts!

Diana is the hero of this story. But behind her is a parent who encouraged her. As a parent—or even a mentor or a confidant to a young person—you can make a difference by sharing your knowledge of speaking and giving them the gentle push they need to start speaking. After they gain the courage to "cross their own rivers," they will wave back to you with gratitude from the other side.

PowerSpeaking®
First Graders? Absolutely!

Each year our company awards three people the "Golden Mic Award" to acknowledge their use of communication skills. Pauline Binkley was one of the award winners in 1992 for her work with her first graders. It all got started when we received a couple of letters:

July 28, 1992

Dear Mr. Gilbert,

In October of '91, I had the good fortune to be in the audience at Nordstrom Walnut Creek when you presented *"The Power of Speaking: From Boredom to Impact."*

I was chosen to be an active participant and you handed me a set of tapes which I have listened to several times.

After your presentation, I decided to teach "PowerSpeaking" to my first-grade class. Since I was being evaluated in the spring by my principal, I had him come in to hear the children speak. He was so taken by what he had heard and seen that he stayed to listen to all thirty speeches and wrote the enclosed note in addition to a great evaluation of my professional skills.

Thank you so much for the tapes and the impetus to constantly improve my teaching. The children and I are grateful.

Sincerely,
Pauline Binkley

Letter to Pauline from her principal, Bill Senning:

April 28, 1992

Dear Pauline,

You know, if anyone asked me, I'd tell them that you just couldn't teach first-graders to do what I saw this morning. I was a speech minor in college and I'm not sure all my classmates could do this.

In the eight years that I've known you, I've admired you for your willingness to challenge the assumptions, to combat the myths we may have contrived over the years.

There are probably a lot of people who would say that six-year-olds are too young to learn "power speaking," but your kids knew gestures, posture, projection, eye contact and they knew how to do it.

Hey, you're damned good!

Bill

Pauline teaches at Gomes Elementary School in Fremont, California. In 1988-89 Gomes received the prestigious National Elementary School Recognition Award as an outstanding model of high-quality education. The award was presented by President Reagan to Principal William Senning.

Here are Pauline's comments from the Golden Mic Awards and the short speeches of two of her star pupils.

"I fear heights and I fear falling, but a year ago, I would rather bungy jump than be here on this stage tonight. The day after taking a Power-Speaking® workshop though, I got excited about public speaking. Not for me, but for my first grade students. I went on to teach my 30 students to be speakers. Surprisingly, they enjoyed it and each week they couldn't wait to get up to talk. When these kids reach adulthood, they won't be afraid to speak out.

Tonight I have two of my former students who are eager to speak to you."

Jeffrey Tan

"Anyone can get nervous when they speak. Last year Mrs. Binkley taught me never to appear nervous. Anyone can be a Powerspeaker!

When I grow up I want to be a doctor so I can help sick people and I'd like to drive a white Lamborghini."

Amanda Kahn

"I would like to be three things when I grow up: a paramedic, a lifeguard and a swim teacher. Why I want to be those three things is because I like helping people.

Last year Mrs. Binkley taught me how to PowerSpeak. She taught me how to plant my feet, to look at the audience, project my voice, use large gestures and to have confidence. I love PowerSpeaking."

The Soul
of Speaking

> *"All I do is initiate the structure and the skills, assume the stance and just let go. The creativity emerges with power. It touches lives and heals me . . . and that heals everyone else. One person can make a difference. If we follow our own hearts, we can walk other people along with us."*
> —*Annee Pavlich, R.N.*

Speaking can be exhilarating. Being able to influence how people think, feel and act is a talent that can change the world. It starts with you. It's an inside job. At its essence, speaking is not about style, technique or perfection. It's about you, the speaker.

In this book you have learned a lot about the techniques of effective speaking. But keep in mind, that's only the mechanical part. Far more important is the essence of you and your message.

The articles in this chapter are about the personal aspects of speaking, not the technique. Since at the heart of any great speech is passion, this is the logical place to end.

Divine Dissatisfaction

A wise old sage once said, "There are really three talks: the one you plan to give, the one you give and the one you wish you had given." From the rank beginner to the seasoned professional, speakers are rarely satisfied with their performances. This is as it should be. This "divine dissatisfaction" keeps us striving to make it better next time.

Artists and performers take little comfort in the success of a current piece of work: they're driven by their passion for the next project. Speakers would be well-advised to follow their lead.

"There is a vitality, a life force, a quickening that is translated through you into action. And because there is only one of you in all time, this expression is unique.

If you block it, it will never exist through another medium and will be lost. The world will not have it. It is not your business to determine how good it is, nor how valuable it is, nor how it compares with other expressions. It is your business to keep it yours—clearly and directly; to keep the channel open.

You do not have to ever believe in yourself or your work. Keep the channel open. No artist is pleased. There is no satisfaction at anytime. There is only a queer, divine dissatisfaction—a blessed unrest that keeps us marching and makes us more alive than the others."

—Martha Graham
Dancer

❖ ❖ ❖

"I used to be elated by the success and crushed by the failures. Now I realize it's not the highs and lows that count. It is the work that matters."*

—Paul Simon
Musician
Reflections on the success of "Graceland"
*Paraphrase of a quote from a radio interview

❖ ❖ ❖

"If something goes wrong, I say 'OK, luck of the draw. Maybe next time.' I've watched a lot of people go stark-raving crazy if they push too far—they meet obstacles they can't overcome. I say, 'I'm going to be the best I can and that will be good enough.' The point of my photography isn't to make a sharper picture than everyone else. It's to have emotional content that communicates."

—Galen Rowell
Photographer

❖ ❖ ❖

"I am the way I am; I look the way I look; I am my age."

—Barbara Walters
Journalist

"I've never come off the stage at the end of a performance and said, 'Tonight, everything was perfect." There will always be some little thing that I'll have to get right tomorrow."

—Jessica Tandy
Actress

"My preference among the 35 books I've written is always the next one. I'm an old pro. And the job of a pro is to move on to the next task."

—James Michener
Author

"Security is mostly a superstition. It does not exist in nature, nor do the children of men as a whole experience it. Avoidance of danger is not safer in the long-run than outright exposure. Life is either a daring adventure or nothing."

—Helen Keller
Teacher

"After decades of giving speeches, from five minutes to five days (with breaks!) in length, I've yet to be satisfied with one of them. But tomorrow is another day. Forget the 'This is my only chance to shine' baloney. If you're worth a darn, you'll get lots of chances to shine."

—Tom Peters
Author

Technique + Soul = Impact

There is a new "infomercial" out advertising a video about improving your golf game. What impressed me was how many physical gadgets they use to help the beginner learn to shoot straight. It is all about developing proper technique.

The same can be said of learning to speak effectively. Certain techniques get results, others do not. It is not a mystery what works. Development of technique and style is the foundation of the expressive arts: painting, dance, writing, music, etc. I would add speaking to that list. Without the foundation of technique and style, the presenter does "what comes naturally." What comes naturally is, in most cases, ineffective. Video feedback and professional coaching can speed the development of technique and style. The result is a more powerful presenter.

But this foundation is just the beginning. With only technique and style, the speaker may seem a bit like a robot doing nothing important very well. The other critical ingredient is what I call "soul." Soul is your passion, your commitment, your strong position.

It's been said that speaking before groups is the #1 fear. I don't believe it. I think what we really fear is taking a strong position, speaking with conviction.

Recently, during a large group workshop I conducted, a woman got up and spoke out strongly on the issue of world hunger. Another person commented, "That speech had soul."

It is our willingness to mean what we say, not just be entertaining, that gives our presentations power and humanity.

Paul Horn, the great jazz flute player addressed this issue eloquently:

"At some point in a musician's life and development, his instrument becomes purely a tool, an extension of himself. This is when the theory and the technical problems of the instrument have been overcome and he no longer thinks about them. He's free just to play, to be an open channel to let the creative force within express itself effortlessly through him and his instrument. If all the technical knowledge is now automatic and acting from a subconscious level, what is coming out? The essence of his being, all that he has experienced in life, all the people he has met, all the places he has been and all the sufferings, frustrations and joys. His attitudes, his moral and ethical values and most important, his inner feeling and convictions about God, the master creator."

So as you learn the technique and style of speaking, also reach deep inside for the essence of your reason to speak. The combination will make you a speaker with impact.

Stand Up and Speak Out: Spontaneous Speaking The Oratorical Equivalent of Bungee Jumping

Contributed by Melinda Henning

It happens in a flash of insight. Ideas churning in your mind for weeks crystallize instantaneously into one incisive statement. You're startled to realize you know exactly what to say, and the strength of your conviction propels immediate expression. That's the brand of speaking I admire most: spontaneous speaking. Leaping past your inner critic, you stand up and speak out with both creativity and courage. If you've experienced spontaneous speaking yourself, you know the thrill. For one riveting moment, you trusted your mind and your heart in the presence of others. There definitely is risk: you can't predict reactions. But the reward might be a lasting and positive impact.

An Asian engineer in a high tech company, for example, practicing a speech in a PowerSpeaking® program, circled verbally around his position on the damaging effects of cultural stereotypes. As time ran short, he paused for several seconds. His widening eyes revealed an "ah hah!" of discovery. *"I am asking you to be color blind!"* he finally concluded. *"Color blind. For just one nanosecond."* The image created by those few words contained the essence of his whole speech. And that ending statement wasn't planned. It happened in the pause, and he let it.

In case the term spontaneous speaking reminds you of speaking in tongues, let me clarify. I am not referring to mindless "spouting off," channeling or street corner preaching. *Spontaneous speaking reflects a moment of personal brilliance, when the best in one person's uninhibited brain power and heartfelt energy meet an audience ready to listen.* A rare creative synergy of necessary elements is what makes this communication marvel so deserving of our notice and respect:

- ▶ a quick and elegant combination of previously unconnected thoughts (the mental process);

- ▶ an effortless distillation of these thoughts into a cogent sentence or two (finding the words);

- ▶ a gut-level sense of conviction about your message (emotional energy); and

- ▶ an audience that can understand (an appropriate context).

Spontaneous speaking can occur in the most domestic of settings, in business or academic meetings, at commemorative gatherings—anywhere a group shares a purpose or topic. It may be motivated by righteous indignation, by love, at times by an uncanny sense of humor. Always, though, precisely the right words take life quickly, as if beyond our control. We don't plan this; we just allow it.

Politicians occasionally share moments of spontaneous speaking, although most of their comments are judiciously planned. President Clinton departs from his prepared text, playing off audience interaction, when speaking on something he cares about deeply. It worries his staff. They think of it as "the oratorical equivalent of bungee jumping," according to *Newsweek*. His first State of the Union address announced unequivocally his commitment to comprehensive health care reform (instead of only hinting at it, as in the text). *"All our efforts will fail,"* he intoned, away from the TelePrompTer, *"unless we also take this year—not next year, not five years from now, but this year—bold steps to reform our health-care system."*

Children can be masters of spontaneous speaking. They're less inhibited than adults. One Christmas, my two young sons (then six and eight) and I were baking gingerbread cookies together, and the boys were quizzing me on astrology. They wanted to know what sign they were born under and what the signs meant. (This was at a time when these two pals also wrestled daily with the rivalry typical of their ages, and Ryan, the younger one, chafed frequently under his bigger brother Gavin's bossy directives.) The minute I replied "Cancer" to Gavin's question about his birth sign, Ryan shot like a pogo stick up onto a chair, arm raised and finger pointed in proclamation, punching up every word: *"Scientists have not been able to figure out how to cure cancer!"* We all fell into peals of insightful laughter. (Of course this same good-natured proclamation is offered again, 15 years later, whenever Ryan disagrees with his older brother.)

As in bungee jumping, to feel the thrill, you'll have to be willing to take the risk. Once, my two sons and my partner Richard and I were in a packed movie theater as the film "Dark Man" appeared on the screen. We had hastily chosen this movie from the brief newspaper review, promising a "classic adventure story contrasting archetypes of good and evil." Sounded like wholesome family fare. Yet the first five minutes displayed more consistent, close-up, graphic violence than any normal person would choose to see in a lifetime. I was appalled! All my worries about violence permeating society, all my wishes to stop it surfaced and merged. Without prelude, I stood up and spoke out right from my seat, loudly enough to be heard by the entire balcony: *"I am not going to pay money to support this kind of senseless violence!"* Then to my sons, *"And I certainly am not going to pay money to feed this toxic imagery into the brains of my children!"* I stomped out and demanded a refund at the box office.

My guess is that we've all had such moments of inspiration, when we've suddenly found just the right words to say at just the right time. It's the courage to say them that often is lacking. I want to encourage you to declare your serendipitous insights more often. Let yourself speak out when you're jolted by a rare combination of creativity and conviction. It's worth the risk. That moment when you are moved to speak may be one time your words can make a real difference.

Dad Was a Speaker

Carl's eyes filled with tears. His voice cracked. He lovingly recounted how a high school teacher's influence had stopped him from "becoming a bum." Carl was sharing this heartfelt story with 200 people in my new program, "Fire in the Belly: The Essence of Change." People told me later he was a crusty retired Army colonel who was not noted for being vulnerable like this. When we express the gratitude we feel for mentors who have helped us along the way, we may experience some strong emotion.

My dad was a business speaker. He was in the insurance industry. His territory was the San Francisco Bay Area and Northern California. Before ascending to higher levels of management, he was on the road quite a bit doing business speeches. He even attended night school to enhance his speaking skill.

Only in the past few years have I fully appreciated the enormous influence my dad had on my career direction. He made it clear to me that people who communicate confidently would move ahead. He encouraged this skill in me at an early age. At the drop of a hat, I'd be up showing off for my parents' friends.

In the early days of television, we used to watch the prize fights every Friday from Madison Square Gardens in New York City. Dad would model, then encourage me to get up in the middle of our living room and mimic the announcer. Holding an imaginary microphone in my left hand and raising my right arm straight above my head I'd bellow out: "Laaaaadies and gentlemennnnn, welcome to The Friday Night Fights brought to you by the Gillette Cavalcade of Sports . . ." Growing up, I was never at a loss for encouragement to get up and speak. When I ran for school offices, it was my well-honed speeches that got me elected.

Because of all this, public speaking was never a fearful thing for me. It was an exciting vehicle for self-expression and accomplishment. As a youngster, though, I never imagined it would become my life's work. Clearly, in this aspect of my life, my dad was my mentor.

Later in life, I found out that the mentor relationship is often a two-way affair. My major dissertation supervisor was a psychologist named Bob Suczek. He was both confrontational and supportive during the two years of the most intensive phase of the writing. After the process was over, I wrote him a letter expressing my gratitude. He wrote a note back saying simply, "What you may not have known, Rick, is that I needed you as much as you needed me." Bob Dylan once spoke of his relationship to Woody Guthrie, his musical mentor: "To me he was like a link in a chain, like I am to many others and like we all are to someone. We're all just links in a chain."

Al Pacino won the Oscar for best actor in 1993. In his acceptance speech at the Academy Awards, he touched on the two-way nature of the mentor relationship:

"I've been very lucky. I found desire for what I do early in my life. I'm lucky because I had people who encouraged that desire, from Lee Strasberg, to my great friend and mentor, Charlie Laughton . . . Now, recently, a young girl came up to me

when I was at a function for the South Bronx—
which is where I'm from. She said that I had
encouraged her—not necessarily by my work but
just by the fact that we came from the same place.
I just can't forget that girl and I can't forget the
kids out there who may be thinking tonight, 'If he
can do it, I can do it . . .' I want to thank the
Academy for giving us the gift of encouragement."

So it is . . . we are helped by others and then we
turn around and pass it on. Who have been your
mentors? What were their characteristics? Are they still
alive? Do you need to tell them what influence they
had on your success? I'm sure they would appreciate
hearing from you. Thank you, Dad. Thank you, Bob.

On the other side, is there someone tugging at your
sleeve, asking for your help? Remember, we're all just
links in a chain. Twenty years from now as our
daughter reflects on her mentors perhaps . . . just
perhaps, she'll say, "Dad was a speaker."

The Power of the Hero's Journey

Luke Skywalker is hurtling toward the nuclear reactor of the dreaded Death Star in *Star Wars*. Empire fighters are in hot pursuit. At the last moment, Luke hears Obi-Wan Kenobi say, "Trust the Force," and turns off his guidance computer. He evades his pursuers and blows up the Death Star.

In *The Wizard of Oz*, Dorothy is held prisoner in the castle of the Wicked Witch. An hour-glass measures the minutes she has to live. All hope is gone. Suddenly the image of Auntie Em appears in the crystal ball. Dorothy sobs, "Oh Auntie Em, I'm scared." Back in Kansas, she tells everyone of her adventure and the lesson she learned: "There's no place like home."

Both *Star Wars* and *The Wizard of Oz* follow story lines often seen in the best Hollywood films: that of the "ordinary" hero. Mythologist Joseph Campbell describes the appeal of such stories in *Hero with A Thousand Faces*. Stories of mythic proportions involve life's basic lessons. Typically, the story's main character starts out as an ordinary person. He or she then gets a "call to adventure"—either by choice or by circumstance.

The protagonist leaves the comforts of home and family to begin the journey. Along the way there are life-threatening challenges. Things get worse. Finally, it

215

looks like the end—there's no hope. Then, at the point of greatest despair, the hero finds some inner strength to triumph over the odds. This inner strength is usually the message, or moral, of the story: "Trust the Force," "There's no place like home."

The hero prevails over evil. He or she returns to ordinary life, but with new wisdom. This wisdom is then communicated to the rest of society for everyone's benefit.

Campbell's model helps us understand the value of heroic stories like those of Luke Skywalker and Dorothy. Stories such as these tap into universal human themes. They are used to communicate the basic truths and values we hold dear.

Of what value is this to speakers in business or public life? As you craft stories to use in your speeches, consider the theme of the hero's journey. Topics as wide-ranging in content as altruism for the United Way to quality improvement in industry can fit this pattern. For example, tell how the main character took a risk, struggled against opposition, got in touch with fundamental values (e.g., long-term customer relationships over short-term profits) and helped the company prevail.

By using this storytelling approach, you will tap into a powerful, unconscious reservoir in your audience: the shared experience of overcoming life's hurdles, of striving to excel. And when your stories touch this, your audience will not only hear your message, they will *remember* it—as with the lessons we learn from the best-loved stories.

"Trust the force, Luke. Trust the force."

Using Video to Capture Family History

We live in a fast-paced world where family ties are not what they used to be. Television and telecommunication cause our attention to be focused in the immediate present. All this may cause us—and our children—to lose touch with our personal histories. If you have an aging parent, grandparent or any important family member and a video camera, you have a unique opportunity to preserve some of this family history.

My father is 88 and my daughter, Kate, is 2-1/2 years old. As an adult, she will remember little about her paternal grandfather. Recently I used the medium of video to preserve for her not only our family history, but also a visual experience of him. In the interview I did, I asked my dad to comment on such things as: his family; his career history; how he met my mother; his religious and political beliefs; reflections on the big events during his lifetime, i.e., the Depression and World War II. I also asked him what has been most satisfying about his life; what are his regrets; and what would he do differently. Finally, I asked him what advice about life he would have for his granddaughter.

If you want to make a similar tape of someone in your family, here are some tips that might help.

Camera—I used full-sized VHS because it is universal, but small-format cameras can also work well. The advantage of the smaller size is ease of transport.

Tripod—Essential. Use a tripod heavy enough to steady the camera.

Microphone—To get good sound quality, you will need an external clip-on mic and a long cord—about 25 feet. Clip the mic onto your subject's shirt or blouse about four inches below the chin. Connect the other end of the cord into the "external microphone" jack on your camera.

Be sure to do a sound check by recording some footage and playing it back on your camcorder or VCR. Some cheaper mic cords can produce a buzz or hum that will ruin the sound quality.

Lighting—This is critical. Put your subject near a window to get good natural light. Early morning or late afternoon light will give pleasant warmth to your video.

Camera Position—Place your camera about 15 to 20 feet from your subject. Use a variety of long, medium and close shots. Don't be afraid to use tight close ups—let his or her face fill the whole frame—especially for more emotional material.

Your Position—If someone is available to operate the camera for you, sit next to your subject, as on a talk show. Have him or her talk to both you and the camera. If you have no one to operate the camera, sit next to the person for a while, then behind the camera for a while. This will allow you to re-focus the camera for close-ups and will also cause your subject to "talk to the camera."

Interview Content—What your family member talks about is, of course, the most important aspect of the filming. The who, what, when, where and why of the life being profiled is what you are leaving behind for the next generation.

You will choose the content that is most appropriate for your family. However, for a meaningful video record, your purpose should be to get your subject to reflect on things they care about (as well as you). A 45-minute format seemed about right.

I wish I'd started this earlier and had a lot more such tapes—but this is a start. We are now planning to do similar interviews with Kate's maternal grandparents.

My daughter may not understand the importance of this tape until she is well into her twenties. Then she may appreciate the challenges her grandfather faced growing up in a large family with little money, working through the Depression and rising to senior management positions in his company with no college degree. She may also feel a connection to him when he says succinctly at the end of the interview, "With what I had, I did all right."

"When I was a kid starting out in Spokane in the insurance business, the big insurance offices were in San Francisco. I thought, 'Boy, that would be some place to reach for!' I did reach for it and I got it."

—Fred Gilbert

The Truth Is in the Attic

Childhood memorabilia can be enlightening. Preparing for a family reunion recently, I brought down from the attic some dusty shoeboxes filled with old photos, letters and even report cards. I was amused to discover early tendencies that would grow into a life's work. Not all my teachers applauded the junior keynote speaker and trainer that was developing before their eyes. Direct quotes from these report cards:

1st Grade: "His behavior, aside from constant talking, is satisfactory."

2nd Grade: "He could help the whole group by trying harder to control his talking."

3rd Grade: "Ricky is a happy, well-adjusted child. He makes friends easily and has many. He is interested in doing his work and doing it well, but he has so much to say to so many people that he causes a great deal of confusion before and during a lesson."

Sigmund Freud once said: "The boy is father to the man." And so it was. Explore those old shoeboxes. You may find in your past keys to understanding your present. Carl Jung once noted that: "The most important challenge of mid-life is the question, 'What is my story?' "

"Would You Say a Few Words About Dan?"

Contributed by Bill Jacobsen

When the family asks you to deliver a twenty-minute eulogy or to participate in the sharing portion of a memorial service, the following guidelines may help you speak healing words.

- ▶ Share vivid, specific memories of Dan. His beloved idiosyncrasies and foibles will be recognized by everyone in the room. If you evoke laughter along with tears, you are helping the family to say its good-byes.

- ▶ Let Dan be Dan. Don't pretend Dan was a saint. Avoid the maudlin, saccharine, pious or sentimental. Honor the integrity of Dan's life story, its texture and tone. Dishonesty is the worst form of disrespect.

- ▶ Focus on the themes of Dan's personal life story—not on a detailed resume of where he went to school or the positions he held in the corporation or how he died. (It doesn't matter whether he lingered in the intensive care unit for several weeks or committed suicide. Let the medical records reflect how he dies; let *The New*

York Times list his degrees, honors and accomplishments.) You want the quality of Dan's life-long personality to shine through you. Talk about the Dan you remember and love and admire.

▶ Don't flaunt your own religious opinions or think up reasons to justify Dan's death. The worst I've heard: "Dan was so good that God felt he had learned all there was to learn in life. That's why God took him at this time." Accept the fact that family and friends may feel Dan's untimely death isn't fair. Never argue with feelings of rage or dismay.

▶ As you genuinely reveal the Dan you know and respect, he will come to life for a while so close friends and family can complete unfinished conversations with him. This enables the officiant to create an empowering service for the family.

A Living Memorial
for Lauren

In January of 1991 a colleague and friend, Lauren Shrive, lost her battle with cancer. Many of us in the National Speakers Association felt her loss deeply. What we did just prior to her death helped to ease her pain . . . and ours.

In her final months Lauren was too weak to have many visitors. Friends did the traditional things like call or send cards and flowers. But people felt frustrated at not being able to connect with her personally. We came up with a unique idea: making a videotape for Lauren. That process not only gave her love and support, it gave the rest of us a vehicle to share our feelings and caring with Lauren directly.

It has always seemed to me such a waste that we wait until a friend is gone before we eulogize them. Why not do it while they're still alive? The videotape for Lauren gave us that chance.

During one of our NSA meetings, it was announced that we had a video camera set up for anyone who wanted to say something directly to Lauren after the meeting. The response was overwhelming. People crowded into the room and even waited in the hall to get on the tape. One by one they shared their love with

Lauren via the magic of video. Some laughed, some cried, some spoke of God.

Twenty-six people spoke on the tape, which lasted just under an hour. I sent the tape, unedited, to Lauren the next day, via Federal Express. Later she confided that over the next three days she watched it four times. She made visitors sit down and watch it. She showed it to the visiting-care nurse, to the hospice worker—and most importantly to her family.

She said her family never understood what she did for a living. They did not know exactly what it meant to be a speaker, a trainer, a consultant. And they did not know how many people cared about her. They watched the video and found out.

After she saw the videotape, Lauren suggested I write about the process. She felt others might someday want to use the idea of the videotape "living memorial."

If there is someone in your life who is suffering from a terminal illness, you might consider bringing together friends, associates or even family members to make a video eulogy. All it takes is a video camera, a tripod and an external, clip-on microphone. What people say on camera can be of great comfort to the dying person as well as to those left behind to mourn their loss.

Contributors' Biographies

Talya Bauer

Talya is a Doctoral candidate in Human Resource Management at Purdue University, Indiana.

Wally Bock

Wally is a former FGA board member, a professional speaker and an expert on online research. You may reach him at 800-648-2677 or e-mail to Compuserve 71260,3150 or wbock@holonet.net.

Diana Bonet

Diana is a communications consultant, speaker and writer. She specializes in business and technical writing training and in teaching listening skills. She is the author of six books, including *The Business of Listening*, published by Crisp Publications.

(916) 644-0389

Carol Fleming, Ph.D.

Twenty-five years in the speech changing business, Carol knows how to develop communication skills for the real world. She is the author of "The Sound Of Your Voice," a six-cassette volume published by Simon & Schuster.

(415) 391-9179

Patricia Fripp, CPAE

Patricia is a past president of National Speakers Association. Speech topics include change, teamwork and customer development.

(415) 753-6556

Frederick Gilbert, Ph.D.

Rick is president of Frederick Gilbert Associates, Inc. and developer of PowerSpeaking®. Keynote speeches to corporate and association groups include: "From Boredom to Impact: The Power of Speaking" and "Fire In The Belly: The Essence Of Change."

(415) 368-3699

Melinda Henning

Melinda is a trainer with Frederick Gilbert Associates, Inc. Through her own company, Melinda also does training and consulting on Doing Business By Phone™.

(415) 369-2255

Bill Jacobsen

Bill is the executive director of the Humanist Community, the Humanist Chaplain at Stanford University and the field director of the American Humanist Association.

(415) 969-3630

Jerry Johnson

Jerry counsels people through life and job transitions. He is a vice president at Drake Bean Moran, an outplacement firm in San Francisco. Jerry was in the broadcasting industry for sixteen years with ABC and is a past president of the Northern California chapter of the National Speakers Association.

(415) 986-3532

Steve Kirsch

Steve is founder and vice president of Frame Technology in San Jose, CA. Frame produces computer publishing software.

(408) 922-2708

Mary McGlynn

Mary is a partner and trainer with FGA. Mary specializes in women's presentation issues.

(415) 368-3699

Robert Middleton

Robert is a marketing consultant, copywriter and workshop leader.

(415) 956-3789

Lu Ellen Schafer

A speaker and trainer, Lu Ellen helps companies communicate effectively with their foreign-born employees.

(408) 423-1339

Steve Schramm

Steve is the director of communication engineering at General Magic in Mountain View, CA.

(415) 966-6268

Maureen Sullivan

Maureen is the owner of a diet center called Lite for Life in Burlingame, California.

(415) 941-8096

John Warren

John believes "There Is Always A New Twist" and uses creative thinking for problem solving and team-building for companies and associations. He has been a trainer with Frederick Gilbert Associates, Inc. for many years.

(415) 345-4408

Jeffrey Wildfogel, Ph.D.

Jeffrey consults and speaks on leadership, productivity and sales and teaches *The Psychology of Peak Performance* at Stanford University. He also does one-on-one coaching to help people achieve their dreams.

(415) 948-9200

Give the Gift of PowerSpeaking® to Your Friends and Colleagues

ORDER FORM

YES, I want _____ copies of *PowerSpeaking®: How Ordinary People Can Make Extraordinary Presentations* at $19.95 each, plus $3 shipping per book (California residents please add $1.65 state sales tax per book). Canadian orders must be accompanied by a postal money order in U.S. funds. Allow 30 days for delivery.

☐ **YES**, I am interested in learning more about the PowerSpeaking® programs. Please send information.

My check or money order for $_____ is enclosed.

Name _____ Phone _____

Organization _____

Address _____

City/State/Zip _____

Check your leading bookstore or
Make your check payable and return to:

Frederick Gilbert Associates, Inc.
1233 Harrison Ave
Redwood City, CA 94062